Cannabis for Couples

"If you've ever imagined that there might be a kind older person with decades of personal and professional experience on how to best use cannabis, who would share in depth a multitude of ways to improve your experiences, you're going to want this book. John Selby is all of the above and a lot more. This book will lead you into more pleasure, more awareness, greater depths, more sensory excitement, more fun, and more wisdom. Spoiler alert: the last few chapters take what you've learned from the rest to a whole new level. Consider this book to be a gift to yourself, your partner, and your relationship."

JAMES FADIMAN, PH.D.,
AUTHOR OF *THE PSYCHEDELIC EXPLORER'S GUIDE*
AND COAUTHOR OF *YOUR SYMPHONY OF SELVES*

"John Selby's years of experience supporting couples on their journey of intentional cannabis use shines throughout this wonderful book. Sharing the cannabis space with a partner is a deeply meaningful experience—and rich with connection and depth. When used intentionally, cannabis can bring couples together in ways that are truly magical. John's teachings are sincere, incredibly skillful, and pragmatic. He takes all of the trial and error out of the equation, and this allows couples to immediately benefit from safe and sacred cannabis use. He outlines a wonderful foundation that can support years of sacred intimacy between loving partners. I highly recommend this book."

DANIEL MCQUEEN, EXECUTIVE DIRECTOR
OF THE CENTER FOR MEDICINAL MINDFULNESS
AND AUTHOR OF *PSYCHEDELIC CANNABIS*

"John Selby has provided a higher education for couples. His chapter on marijuana and sex, 'Tapping Eros Transformation,' is a true gift, especially for couples transitioning into middle age or beyond. With specific exercises designed to deepen intimacy, this book makes plain how cannabis can make love bloom anew. One can only imagine what such rarely spoken of information can do for a couple in their 20s or 30s! I highly recommend it!"

CHARLES WININGER, LP, LMHC,
AUTHOR OF *LISTENING TO ECSTASY*

"John Selby's new book is an excellent guide for couples considering bringing cannabis into their lives or expanding the range of their current use. The guidance is also just as useful for individuals looking for reliable, extensively 'field-tested' information. The book covers all the important bases, is direct and intimate in tone, and chock-full of accessible suggestions, checklists, affirmations, and anecdotes. I'm confident that reading *Cannabis for Couples* and putting the information to use will revitalize many a relationship. And, again, it's not just for couples."

STEPHEN GRAY, EDITOR OF *CANNABIS AND SPIRITUALITY*

"Do you and your partner want to take your relationship to a whole new dimension of ecstatic interaction? Are you open-minded enough not to be bothered about our culture's mostly foolish admonitions against a simple, completely natural herb like cannabis? If so, here's a simply great guided program for you and yours on how to elevate your intimacy. Highly recommended!"

WILL JOHNSON, AUTHOR OF
CANNABIS IN SPIRITUAL PRACTICE

Cannabis for Couples

Enhance Intimacy and Elevate Your Relationship

JOHN SELBY

Park Street Press
Rochester, Vermont

Park Street Press
One Park Street
Rochester, Vermont 05767
www.ParkStPress.com

Text stock is SFI certified

Park Street Press is a division of Inner Traditions International

Cataloging-in-Publication Data for this title is available from the Library of Congress

ISBN 978-1-64411-041-6 (print)
ISBN 978-1-64411-042-3 (ebook)

Printed and bound in the United States by Lake Book Manufacturing, Inc.
The text stock is SFI certified. The Sustainable Forestry Initiative® program
promotes sustainable forest management.

10 9 8 7 6 5 4 3 2 1

Text design and layout by Priscilla Baker
This book was typeset in Garamond Premier Pro with Botany and Nexa used as
display typefaces

To send correspondence to the author of this book, mail a first-class letter to the
author c/o Inner Traditions • Bear & Company, One Park Street, Rochester, VT
05767, and we will forward the communication, or contact the author directly at
www.johnselby.com.

The muse of marijuana is valuable and trustworthy
to share together with your loved one
when approached mindfully
and with an open heart.

A Cautionary Note to the Reader

This book is intended as an informational guide. The approaches and techniques described herein should not be seen as an endorsement to use marijuana. Although marijuana has become legal in many states, the purity of some of the available products is still inconsistent. Please use caution when using vaping products, edibles, and other forms of cannabis.

Contents

Acknowledgments

All relationships are a
transformative experience.
Intimacy creates understanding,
and understanding creates love.

Many people have helped me create this book and my *Cannabis for Couples* programs. I especially want to thank my early mentors and teachers: Krishnamurti and Humphry Osmond, Alan Watts and Chuck Kelly, Rebecca Oriard and Ralph Abraham, and Osho and Rico – plus the research team at the Bureau of Research in Neurology and Psychiatry in Skillman, New Jersey. I was so often blessed with helpful guides whose wise insights permeate this book.

I also want to thank the many friends who explored all the various dimensions of marijuana with me and my clients and students over the years and revealed their personal insights and experiences with it.

And finally, as always, a million thanks to my partner, Birgitta Steiner, who both inspired this book and infused it with her poems, her special understanding of the cannabis muse, and her nonstop adventurous spirit. Also, a very special nod of appreciation to Jesse Smith and the tech team who created the Mindfully High app that accompanies this book, and to Paul Benedict for all his essential contributions.

*Through giving and receiving
unconditionally while high
and letting our hearts lead the way,
we can connect soul to soul
and respond in new ways
that bring delightful surprises.*

*As the muse of marijuana
stimulates inner harmony,
may we experience a joy
that goes beyond happiness,
originating from deep within
and radiating outward into
new expressions of intimacy.*

How Cannabis Enhances Intimacy

By openly sharing your intimate
feelings and sudden intuitions,
you transform the mundane
into vast realms of newness.

By surrendering to emotional authenticity,
you can embrace each other unconditionally
and express your compassion
spontaneously.

By balancing your emotions
while keeping your heart open,
you can generously give comfort
and provide your loved one
with nurturing support.

All human cultures are built on the foundation of deep emotional bonding between two loving people. This intimate level of relating has always been the bedrock of our survival, economic success, and emotional fulfillment. But . . . what happens when we introduce the powerful and mostly untested ingredient of cannabis into the complex and intimate couple's experience?

Just two generations ago, only the far fringe of our culture was using cannabis. Now over half of America's adult population openly admits in surveys that they've tried marijuana. According to a 2017 Yahoo poll, thirty-five million Americans enjoy cannabis regularly, and another twenty million use it occasionally. More than twelve million American couples say that they use cannabis to enhance their intimate experiences, with ten million more expected to do the same in the next few years. In fact, more than seven thousand people try marijuana for the first time every day.

So we certainly need to ask: how does cannabis impact a loving relationship – and how can couples approach cannabis to maximize benefits while minimizing potential downsides?

Depending on several variables, pot can make us feel stoned and relatively unconscious or high and acutely conscious. Can we mindfully use this natural herb to expand consciousness, rather than collapse it, when we're with our loved one? Specifically, can we get high together in ways that actively and predictably enhance our relationship?

There are hundreds of new books teaching us how to raise, market, cook, and ingest this powerful herb. But thus far very few books offer couples professional guidance, information, insight, and advice for integrating cannabis into their intimate relating. It's time for full in-print transparency regarding the ways in which grass can influence our love life.

Whether you already use it with your loved one, you've been seriously considering it, or you're just beginning to look into it, I'm writing this book to, I hope, answer the questions you might have concerning cannabis as an aid to your relationships.

In this book we aim to unveil the mysteries regarding the use of cannabis by couples. We'll definitely look closely at situations where using marijuana unwisely might hinder romance and deep heart-to-heart bonding – because cannabis is a powerful and sometimes unpredictable force to insert into our lives. But mostly we'll be looking at how the mindful use of cannabis can elicit a truly wonderful shared sense of inner release, well-being, pleasure, communion, and awakening. Even though our government has mostly inhibited research into this herb, we do, in fact, already know a great deal about the predictable impact of marijuana on a couple's intimate relating.

THE CANNABIS REVOLUTION

In the late 1960s, even before I was out of college, I received a sociology grant from the National Institutes of Health (NIH) to conduct a detailed survey of marijuana usage on the Princeton University campus, and also a parallel survey in New York City. The results shocked the Princeton administration because we discovered that over half of the students regularly using grass were on the dean's list for academic excellence – which was the exact opposite of what had been anticipated.

Back then, academic research on cannabis was mostly forbidden under penalty of very harsh laws. A small minority of us happened to stumble on the positive psychological power of marijuana, but we also ran headlong into remarkably repressive, fear-based, societal judgments, plus long prison sentences if we were caught with even a pipeful of the forbidden herb. Nevertheless, for three decades after graduate school, working as a couples therapist, first with the Presbyterian Church and then independently, I joined a number of therapists quietly recommending marijuana as a safe and helpful ingredient to resolve personal conflicts and nurture a couple's intimate life.

> Only recently has science caught up with what therapists have known for decades – cannabis usually helps people feel less anxious and more open to exploring otherwise uncharted realms of intimate relating.

We're currently living through a long-awaited cannabis-stimulated cultural revolution – one that many of us had given up hope would ever happen in America, at least during our lifetime. Over the last decade, the long-standing societal and government repression has begun to dissipate, and average Americans are finally able to explore the quite remarkable powers awaiting us within the tetrahydro-cannabinol (THC) molecule – one of the main psychoactive constituents. Almost overnight, we've seen both medical and social experts reverse course to praise the potential of cannabis to improve our lives.[1] Even conservative corporations, such as Molson Coors Brewing Company (which recently announced its intention to produce a line of beer infused with cannabis extracts), are looking for ways to make marijuana a mainstream product.[2]

> We've now reached the historic point where many millions of American couples are welcoming the marijuana muse into their relationships, and millions more are ready to jump in and explore the impact of cannabis in their personal lives, without the fear of societal retribution.

The media continues to present us with general headlines about the positive power that marijuana packs for enhancing such things as self-confidence, creative expression, and erotic pleasure. Recent studies at Stanford and elsewhere have documented that over two-thirds of the American couples using pot say that it definitely boosts their sexual engagement.[3] Furthermore, new research indicates that couples who use cannabis are more likely to stay happily together, compared to couples who do not use it.[4]

Now that marijuana has been proven to help reduce social anxiety, boost empathy, relieve depression, heighten sensory pleasure, and increase libido, a great many couples are saying, well, why not try it? If they already use it, they're considering ways to explore added intimate dimensions stimulated by its effects. You yourself have picked up this book almost certainly because you're curious about how the muse of marijuana might benefit your current relationship, or perhaps your next intimate involvement.

Cannabis for Couples will provide you with trustworthy and practical information, guidance, and insights, gathered from actual hands-on experience with couples exploring the power of the marijuana muse.

SEVEN HIGH DIMENSIONS

Beyond popular media articles and still-incomplete scientific reports, exactly what happens when two people get high together? Are there hidden dangers you should learn to avoid? Does cannabis stimulate predictable types of experience and behavior? Most importantly, how can these experiences be approached creatively in order to positively impact your relationship?

To begin answering these questions, let's first take a look at the seven primary dimensions of the cannabis experience, each of which can impact intimate relating. Regardless of whether you're new to grass or have a long history with the herb, you'll find that each of these core dimensions, when approached wisely, can enhance your desire for shared adventure, bonding, and fulfillment.

It doesn't matter if you're straight or gay, liberal or conservative, young or old, rich or not so rich. When you explore these seven dimensions of cannabis with your partner, you'll discover new meaningful opportunities opening up.

You may find that you naturally flow through these seven different dimensions in order, so that they seem more like phases of the cannabis experience. Or you may not – you may move through them in a different order, or you may experience some but not all of them.

I was originally introduced to this way of viewing the marijuana experience by professor Charles Tart, and I remain deeply thankful to him for all his great research.[5] Throughout this book, we'll be delving deeper into these seven dimensions, one by one.

1. *Conjuring the muse* (preparing for a cannabis experience)
2. *Tapping THC magic* (partaking of the herb together)
3. *The pot chatter buzz* (enjoying a unique "talking rush")
4. *Enhanced sensation* (opening to pure sensory pleasure)
5. *Eros transformation* (shifting into a deep sexual interlude)
6. *Creative insight* (exploring breakthrough realizations)
7. *Mutual awakening* (meditating – "tripping" together)

Most couples I've worked with say that when they are high together, they experience these seven stages in their relating. However, please don't expect your experience to necessarily follow any set order each time you get high with your partner. Probably the best thing about getting high is that it's always new – you never know what's going to happen because it's always a unique moment-to-moment experience. Why? Because cannabis ingestion temporarily turns off most of your future projections and likewise shuts off the lights on recent past experiences.

With all that shut off, and all your senses temporarily boosted, you're naturally just right here in the present moment, rather than constantly comparing your present experience with associations from the past and projections into the future. This cannabis mind-set is liberating for most people – it's the "Ahhh" moment when suddenly you realize that you're fully alive in the now – and what's more, it feels very good. If pot is at all psychologically addictive, it's because this "newness" dimension is always a relief, an open window into freshness, an opportunity to discover untapped insights. The trick is to enter into this flow of unique experience mindfully and, in my opinion, thankfully.

By the way, this progression of the cannabis experience for couples applies equally well to platonic friendships without any sexual dimensions. Six of the seven dimensions of a shared marijuana adventure are important in both platonic friendships and romantic involvements, which means that you can apply most of the suggestions in this book to whatever friendship you choose. By having a shared understanding and general intent when you get high with a friend, you'll be able to delve more deeply into new shared insights.

LETTING GO . . . AND TRUSTING

Although most of these seven dimensions of the "couples high" will make an appearance one way or another almost every time you use cannabis with your loved one, it's not really possible to predict and manipulate the high experience. Instead, as I learned from my early mentor Humphry Osmond, a British psychiatrist and pioneer in the field of psychedelics research, with whom I conducted several research projects at the New Jersey Neuro-Psychiatric Institute, there's an elusive and ephemeral pervading influence that seems to guide and inform each new cannabis adventure. Humphry called this guiding influence "the marijuana muse" and recommended that everyone using marijuana trust and flow with this inner intuitive guidance.[6]

Cannabis strongly impacts consciousness with a unique, ephemeral, impish, and often delightful swirl of new experience and insight.

Because your usually authoritarian ego can't dominate and control the marijuana muse, a certain special quality of inner trust is required in order for you to let go and flow freely with the cannabis high. Put bluntly: getting high means temporarily surrendering ego control of your inner focus and intent and just relaxing enjoyably into whatever naturally transpires between you and your partner.

Everyone who gets high is, in fact, asking for this invisible muse to come and tap them with its magic wand and stimulate a transcendent inner experience. Perhaps this is the main lure and payoff of using cannabis – it sets us free from our habitual ego-control patterns so that we can once again (like we did as little kids) experience each moment as qualitatively new and intriguing.

We all know that mundane reality is often repetitive and uneventful and sometimes downright boring or upsetting. Even when we're with someone we really like and resonate with, we can stay stuck in habitual thoughts, constricted feelings, and defensive behaviors. All of us are often victims of our own routines and inhibitions. This is the reason that we seek periodic moments of transcendence, when the dominance of the thinking, plotting, worrying mind drops temporarily away and we're suddenly free to expand our consciousness in fun and rewarding directions.

Tapping into such magical transcendent moods can happen spontaneously, of course, when we suddenly, for no reason at all, feel really good inside our own skin. Sometimes yoga or jogging or dancing, or encountering beauty in any form, can make our heart leap and sing for joy. As you perhaps already know, alcohol also can shift some of us into a short transcendent state, although usually with negative side effects. A business breakthrough, creative realization, or sexual rush can also transport us into temporary bliss.

The marijuana muse offers yet another way in which we can actively transcend the humdrum and self-inflicted emotional suffering that we find in everyday existence.

BEYOND OLD PROGRAMMINGS

In our society, especially in religious circles, many of us grew up in communities that seriously frowned on seeking pleasure for pleasure's sake. The traditional Protestant work ethic made people feel guilty for just kicking back and enjoying the beauty and bliss found in the present moment. We were supposed to stay continually busy and productive – "an idle mind is the devil's playground," we heard.

A lot of the 1960s counterculture youth revolution was a reaction to too much seriousness and not enough freedom and fun. Back then, the very idea of using a chemical helpmate like cannabis to induce a temporary sense of transcendence was judged as a crutch or even a sin and rejected. But is this, in fact, a fair judgment?

After observing for decades how the use of weed impacts average lives in divergent ways, I'm personally not an advocate of indiscriminate overindulgence in cannabis. Quite the contrary, actually, because I've seen firsthand a great deal of suffering, loss, delusion, confusion, and downright disaster caused by overmuch dependence on marijuana.[7] Like any other powerful force, cannabis has the potential to encourage growth and pleasure and also to hamper or even damage a person's life.

However, over forty years and counting, my observation is that marijuana's mental and emotional impacts are about 90 percent positive and 10 percent negative. I admit that I'm a die-hard optimist by both temperament and choice – and therefore I'm quite hopeful that increased use of cannabis in our world culture, when approached mindfully and responsibly, will help human beings everywhere on the planet to be more patient, compassionate, understanding, and open-minded toward each other and our ecological future.

Encouraging this positive inner mental, emotional, and spiritual shift by whatever means seems to be humankind's final hope. Either we consciously do something to let go of our programmed greed, hostility, anxiety, delusion, and depression, or we're going to be sunk quite soon. And here's the thing – true revolution always begins in the heart and mind of one person, and then two, and then more, spreading outward into positive group action.

So . . . let's now put our focus on you as an individual, and you as a couple, and see how cannabis might expand and enlighten your relationship and also radiate outward to positively touch your circle of family, friends, and community.

ONE

Meet the Marijuana Muse

Through setting a clear intent to honor and explore the cannabis muse, you can venture beyond the obvious and awaken unlimited possibilities that nourish your relationship.

Imagine two people setting aside an hour or two to be alone together, get high, and just . . . see what happens. Perhaps they chat a bit beforehand about their anticipations and intentions, about their needs and desires, sharing what they might want to experience. Or maybe they just light up or ingest their preferred cannabis product and jump right in.

In either case, these two people are entering into an agreement, even if unspoken, to spend time together under the influence of a consciousness-altering herb. And no one can predict what's going to happen when they get high. It's always new – that's one of the remarkable features of cannabis. You and your partner are opening up to the unexpected, to newness, to emerging opportunities, and who knows, maybe to an encounter with aspects of yourselves that you habitually keep well hidden.

Getting high together is always an adventure, and also
somewhat of a risk for both of you. Grass reduces
social inhibitions; it makes you more honest and
therefore more vulnerable.

When you share marijuana with another person, one of the fundamental assumptions is that you are both willing to take a risk – to become more exposed and open as you venture into unknown realms together. This is an intimate act in and of itself. When you decide to light up or ingest together and focus on each other's presence rather than drift off into solitary zones, you're expressing your willingness to really see your partner, and also to be more fully seen. This is part of the built-in revelatory rush of getting high together.

During my years as a counselor in Hawaii, I worked with a couple named Jim and Danielle. At that point in my career, with steady income from writing self-help books and teaching meditation courses, I'd put aside my formal psychotherapy shingle. Instead, I was working with clients more as a spiritual counselor, shifting from helping emotionally disturbed people find balance to helping relatively normal people expand their inner experience and relationship potential.

Both Danielle and her husband were teachers at the local high school. She came to me first as a meditation student and then as a private client. After a few sessions, she told me she was thinking of leaving Jim because they were no longer finding any real joy in their relationship. Jim had no interest in seeking help from marriage counseling, so she was learning meditation to help her tolerate her current, rather lonely situation.

Jim had smoked pot back in college but had stopped when he got his first teaching job. Danielle had never tried it, but she said that Jim was now getting high most evenings alone in his study. I suggested that she join him and see if the muse of marijuana might open up their relating. She was a bit apprehensive, having been indoctrinated as a child to believe that marijuana was bad and dangerous. However, I gave her my positive perspective on cannabis, and she became more interested, especially when I explained how the marijuana high sometimes runs parallel to and awakens meditative insights.

Danielle told me later that when Jim heard of her interest in getting high with him, he was both surprised and pleased – and he agreed to show up at my office to further discuss this possibility. When I had them both there, I explained how the cannabis high could be approached in a mindful manner with another person. As it turns out, Jim already knew a bit about mindfulness meditation. He'd always seen using marijuana as a solitary retreat into blissful oblivion, not a shared experience – but he was open.

As I explained to them, relating at any level is all about focusing attention outward in the direction of your partner. Learning to finesse this power of compassionate attention is important in any couples experience.

I watched Jim and Danielle eye each other and then look away – but then they looked at each other again and smiled slightly. "So you really want to get high with me?" I remember him asking her. "Well, maybe," she replied tentatively. "If you want to." This made Jim frown. "You've always rejected that part of me," he told her. "I know," she said right back. "But like I told you, John thinks maybe getting high together might wake us up to each other again."

Jim looked at me with a question in his eye. "You're the meditation expert," he said, "and you're encouraging people to get stoned?" I shook my head. "No," I said. "There's a difference between getting stoned and getting high. We get *stoned* to zone out and disappear from the world. As I use the word, we get *high* to tune in to the world and explore new realms of relating. I'm recommending the latter."

Jim and Danielle decided to experiment and see how using cannabis might affect their relationship. Jim wanted to just go home and jump into the experience, but I suggested that they first learn some simple steps to help aim their exploration in rewarding directions. Here are the basics of what I told them.

CONJURING THE MUSE

Whenever two people set aside time to enjoy the muse of marijuana, they're participating in a ritual – they're doing something together that has meaning for them. The act of partaking in the holy herb represents a shared willingness to discover whatever the muse is ready to bring forward at that moment. But even though the experience is always new, the cannabis muse is also highly responsive to the moods and intentions of the couple and to their immediate environment.

Humphry Osmond taught that "set and setting" (mind-set and environment) were crucial to the outcome of a cannabis experience.[1] I explained to Jim and Danielle that this set-and-setting preparation was key to conjuring the marijuana muse because our mood and mind-set as well as our surroundings powerfully influence the type of adventure that cannabis will elicit.

> Psychologically, marijuana definitely makes you more suggestible. This means that you'll tend to get pulled strongly into whatever external situation presents itself to you – so it's important to be mindful of the setting you choose for getting high together.

This doesn't mean you have to micromanage your environment; you simply need to be wise about avoiding situations that will be disturbing or challenging to deal with when you're high. Also, you might choose what music you'd like to listen to together, and whether you want to be in your living room, backyard, bedroom, kitchen, or maybe even the park.

Likewise, you'll want to pause before getting high and note how you're both feeling, mood-wise. You might take a few preliminary quiet moments together to shift into a more relaxed, balanced, positive mind-set so that habitual mental fixations don't stir up unwanted worries and distractions. Toward this mood-balancing end, I taught Jim a basic here-and-now mindfulness process that Danielle was already familiar with (which you'll learn later, and which is found on the High Together app discussed at the end of this book). I suggested that when they were at home, ready to partake together, they set aside five to ten minutes to discuss what they'd like to focus on when they are high, and then to move through the short mindfulness meditation just before lighting up. The fact that they both readily agreed to do this was a good sign for their future together – I could see there was still a spark of attraction and hope between them.

Why is this pause or refocusing step important? Because if you're not in touch with your own inner presence and emotional condition, you can't be present for your partner to relate with.

How you choose to approach the marijuana muse is, of course, up to you and your partner, determined by your current situation and intentions. Step by step, you'll naturally discover your own unique path to ingesting grass together. Certainly, sometimes it's fun to just light up and jump in with zero preparation. But openly talking about your expectations, spending a few quiet moments together to move through a centering process, and then consciously partaking of the herb with clear intent – this approach can add considerably to the experience that emerges.

IN THE BEGINNING

The preliminary process of setting intentions and talking about expectations can be quite informal. Just set aside a few minutes to talk about the general kind of experience you want to move into together. Be sure to let this discussion be free-roaming so that any ideas, insights, memories, and fantasies have the opportunity to emerge.

Danielle and Jim told me later that when they did this, they unexpectedly started talking about things they'd never shared with each other before. They found themselves opening up and exploring shared interests that they'd previously overlooked. Now that they were getting ready to go on an exploration, they found new realms in which to relate.

After talking about expectations, it can be helpful for you and your partner to take a few minutes to focus on being present together – to become grounded, centered, and connected. As you each consciously relax and focus inward, you can observe and accept your current mood and energy level. And as you do this, you can also purposefully expand your bubble of awareness to include your partner in your awareness. Then you're all set to flow together into whatever the muse offers.

As Jim and Danielle told me, after they were done talking, they closed their eyes for a few breaths and listened together to one of my short guided audio programs, which led them inward, step by step, to observe their own current mind-set and emotional condition. Unexpected feelings began to emerge as they let the psychic dust settle, let go of past and future thoughts, and got ready internally to flow into a shared high experience.

This sort of preparation can be seen as an act of respect toward the cannabis muse. Marijuana is definitely a psychoactive drug, especially these days, with strong new strains of cannabis available in many different forms, and respect for the power of the cannabis muse is clearly called for. Just hold in mind that those moments right before you partake are when you determine much of what's going to happen.

Sharing this preparatory moment, before the marijuana high,
will provide both of you with a baseline from which to
observe and guide your inner experience as
the natural chemicals begin to take effect.

Then . . . you smoke, vape, eye-drop, or ingest the herb and commit yourself to being high for at least the next hour or two. You will at some point suddenly feel the transformative influence of THC – and this is always a bit of a jolt to the nervous system – as an altered state of consciousness takes hold of your awareness. By approaching the experience mindfully, as Jim and Danielle did, you won't be caught off guard when the muse of marijuana lifts your awareness up and away into high gear.

THE LEAP OF FAITH

When I talk about the effects of cannabis on human experience, it seems to be almost impossible to avoid using what are commonly called "spiritual" terms. I'm a fairly pragmatic psychologist who no longer identifies with any religious organization or theological belief system. However, this doesn't mean that I don't recognize, respect, and encourage experiences that exist beyond the material limits of scientific understanding.

I did some of my earliest research at Princeton, where Albert Einstein had been a professor for the last decade of his life, and his shaggy ghost seemed to still wander the paths late at night. Einstein once said, "I'm not a religious person, but I am definitely a spiritual person." That pithy quote certainly applies to my experiences with cannabis, which does often awaken deep spiritual experience. In that spirit, I'll be including the more mystic elements of getting high in this discussion – but not within any particular religious framework.

What's key in this regard is realizing that you have the power to aim your mind's focus of attention wherever you want. If you choose to explore meditative, mystic, or religious realms while high, and intently focus in those directions, you'll effortlessly encourage such experiences. As you explore each of the seven dimensions of the cannabis experience that I listed earlier, you will probably discover many opportunities to open up and venture into the more mystic realms of human experience.

That's certainly part of the allure of cannabis – it empowers us to shift into expanded states of mind where we feel more in harmony with the infinity of nature, and with our own deeper nature as well.

Often you'll find that you can't quite verbalize or even think logically about many of the experiences that come to you. Nevertheless, you'll be impacted by them deeply, at both an emotional and an inspirational level. Whatever your personal religious or spiritual inclination, you'll probably find that you can integrate your cannabis-enhanced mystic experiences into your personal belief system. You'll also perhaps discover that your religious beliefs begin to evolve and expand fairly rapidly as a result of using pot mindfully with your loved one.

For several thousand years, as the 1894 *Indian Hemp Drugs Commission Report* documented quite rigorously, cannabis has been accepted and often encouraged in Hindu life as a meditative sacrament.[2] You can still buy cannabis beverages on street corners today in New Delhi. Likewise, many religious sects throughout the world have used psychedelic sacraments to enhance spiritual experience; see my earlier book *Mindfully High* for further discussion of this. But other religions, such as Christianity and Islam, have always been hostile to the use of herbal sacraments to induce mystic experience. I originally trained to be a Presbyterian minister and ran head-on into this prohibition. In the years since, I've worked with many Christian believers who wanted to explore how cannabis might bring them closer to communing with their Creator but, to do so, had to ignore the remonstrations of their minister or hide their use of the herb. Even today, the established Christian churches in America remain hostile to the use of herbal sacraments to stimulate a closer encounter with God.[3]

If the prohibitions of Christianity are an issue for you, let's clear the air right away: It's common knowledge that Jesus made alcohol an integral part of his communion ritual, and alcohol does definitely alter consciousness. Why did my childhood church use grape juice rather than what Jesus prescribed? Perhaps partly to help the alcoholics who come to church for communion, but I suspect the answer is also because when people get high, they temporarily shift beyond any ego-based theological dictums, assumptions, and belief systems and let go of everything they've been taught and programmed to believe – which for a church is dangerous ground indeed.

HIGH SPIRIT

Marijuana definitely serves as a quantum shifter of your usual mind-set, taking you beyond the grip of restrictive one-liner beliefs and ingrained assumptions. As we'll see in more depth later, psychologically, cannabis helps you shift your trust beyond ingrained religious concepts and tight ego control. It encourages you to look directly inward and explore realms of deep spiritual realization beyond the confines of a particular theology.

> When high, you choose to listen to your own inner voice of
> wisdom and truth and to trust in your natural ability
> to open directly to and embrace the universal human
> virtues of compassion, honesty, trust,
> faith, joy, and service.

When you have a mystic experience while relating intimately with your partner, you can share from the depths of your heart and soul. Beyond all the great sexual and psychological insights and encounters that might come to the two of you, there exist deeper realms of intimacy where the muse of marijuana reveals truly remarkable insights and realizations. And these experiences definitely help develop new bonds of togetherness.

I suppose I'm limiting the readership of this book and program by openly talking about spiritual dimensions here at the beginning. However, in the spirit of full transparency, I want to let you know my personal perspective on the value of cannabis at the deeper levels of relating. When you approach the experience of getting high together mindfully, you'll discover that the mundane and the mystic, the physical and the ephemeral, the logical and the transcendent elements of human experience often merge into a greater whole. A higher vision and a most fulfilling shared experience are always waiting. When dealing with something as vast as the human mind, and introducing a chemical that can transform that mind in unpredictable directions, it's important to honor the marijuana muse and approach your experience reverently, in the very best sense of that word.

This is the great joy of cannabis, as well as its great value – it opens us up to new experience, and that's how we grow. And when we share these high experiences, we grow together!

TWO

Clues from the Research Trail

When you trust your own heart,
you generate a deep sense
of inner emotional well-being,
which gives you the freedom
to fully enjoy life's pleasures.

Marijuana will help you
recognize your true nature
as your enthusiasm for the moment
takes you to new heights.

In this chapter, let's pivot our focus and spend a bit of worthwhile time exploring how cannabis affects the mind and body at scientific levels of understanding. In reality, as opposed to media myth, what is marijuana's true biological and psychological nature? What scientific facts about the herb can we state fairly clearly, so that we have a shared understanding of its physical, mental, and emotional impact on our intimate relating?

Sad to say, government-funded marijuana research over the past fifty years has tended to generate quite biased results to satisfy the antidrug funders of that research.[1] I myself got naively involved in a nasty federal NIH data-falsification scheme, and ever since then I've been vigilant about questioning research findings that don't appear valid when compared with actual experience.

In the spirit of seeking honest answers, I'll be drawing the facts and conclusions in this book from formal studies and reports on cannabis that I know can be trusted – for example, the detailed policy paper delivered to the Canadian Senate recently by a team of relatively unbiased scientists.[2]

To begin, cannabis is known by more than 1,200 different names around the world, including marijuana, hemp, pot, weed, or grass. It is a prolific flowering plant that grows naturally throughout most of the world.[3] In fact, throughout the Midwest, many county roads are lined with wild-growing hemp during the summer months.[4] In good soil conditions it can reach as high as twenty feet and may look more like a tree than a weed. Some varieties of the plant have high levels of psychoactive constituents, and some won't get you high at all.

The 2018 U.S. Farm Bill finally made growing certain strains of what's known as "industrial hemp" (which Congress defines as having very low levels of psychoactive constituents) legal in this country. State laws vary on that subject. George Washington himself famously grew great loads of hemp, supposedly using them only for making twine and rope. Indeed, hemp fiber is extremely tough and durable and also serves as excellent fiber for clothing. It's now in vogue again around the world for many manufacturing applications.[5]

The psychotropic (mind-altering) content of the marijuana plant is derived mostly from the bud-like flowers of the female of the species, but in all parts of the plant, even down in the stem, scientists are finding more and more chemicals that appear to be psychoactive or medicinal.[6] More than 520 chemical constituents have been identified in the plant to date. Those that are unique to the plant, of which there are more than eighty, are referred to as cannabinoids.[7]

Cannabis is the only plant on the Earth known to produce two
potent constituents: THC (tetrahydrocannabinol)
and CBD (cannabidiol).[8]

Recent university research has found that a number of cannabinoids have the potential to play with brain chemistry and thus
affect our performance and experience. Many are now being studied
to identify their psychological effects, including cannabinol (CBN),
tetrahydrocannabivarin (THCV), and cannabigerol (CBG). THC
and CBD continue to reign as the most potent stand-alone chemicals;
combining them with other cannabinoids, however, seems to sometimes yield a synergistic effect.

Now that distillation methods can isolate (and deliver for ingestion)
these cannabinoids for medical marijuana products, it's become very
important to determine the particular effects of each one. This research
is still in progress, but it is seriously hindered by the fact that cannabis
remains unjustly classified as a federal Schedule 1 drug. That's the same
category where we find dangerous and addictive drugs such as heroin
and cocaine.[9] However, in contrast to heroin, cocaine, and even other
psychoactive plant materials (such as peyote, psilocybin, and mescaline),
cannabinoids don't contain nitrogen and aren't alkaloids. Marijuana is
neither a strong psychedelic nor physically addictive. In comparison to
other Schedule 1 drugs, it has relatively mild effects.

For decades, the association of cannabis with these other seriously
mind-blowing and addictive drugs has caused untold legal and medical problems. It has also made it very difficult to conduct marijuana
studies on human beings. As more and more states legalize cannabis, I
hope that this antiquated and nonscientific federal legal situation will
be exposed and corrected.

AVAILABLE CANNABIS PRODUCTS

Until recently, the THC content of commercial marijuana ran between
1 and 15 percent. However, over twenty years of selective breeding, in

combination with the development of new distillation and infusion techniques, the percentage of THC in cannabis plants and products has increased greatly.

THC is produced primarily in the flowering bud of the female plant. In fact, the resin secreted by glandular hairs atop the female bud can be up to 90 percent THC. In traditional marijuana cultivation, male and female plants were grown together. However, as soon as a female plant is pollinated by a male plant, the female plant stops secreting resin and shifts into making seeds. When pot growers realized this, they started removing all male plants from their gardens. With no male plants around, the female plants continued to secrete more and more resin, hoping to get pollinated – and the THC content of each bud went up and up and up. Thus was born the *sinsemilla* ("without seed") pot sensation.[10] Thereafter, extremely potent cannabis products became available.

Today, both in marijuana dispensaries and out on the perennial black market, there are many different cannabis products and preparations to choose from.[11] They are typically derived from the flowers and leaves of the traditional Mexican weed (which is low in THC) or the much more potent flowering tips of the sinsemilla plant.

Sometimes you can also buy kief, a potent powder made mostly of trichomes – that is, the hairs and fine outgrowths from the female flower that secrete the cannabinoids (*kief* means "well-being" or "pleasure" in Arabic). Also there's hashish, which is traditionally made from the trichome resin of the female bud, and distilled hash oil, which is mostly pure cannabinoids.[12]

You can also find very potent tinctures, which are alcohol extracts of the raw plant, and infusions that mix hash oil with fats, such as butter or cooking oil, for edible preparations and various pain-relief cosmetics.[13]

Many marijuana products are rated according to their content of THC and CBD. In general, indica strains of cannabis (from the *Cannabis indica* plant) are noted for their high concentration of CBD, while sativa strains (from *C. sativa*) tend to have higher levels of THC. The percentage of THC versus CBD has a strong influence on what type of effect you will experience. CBD tends to have a sedative, analgesic, pain-relieving effect that doesn't get you psychologically high. THC tends to elicit quite definite sensory, cognitive, and sensory alterations, stimulating a quality of consciousness unique to cannabis.

If you and your loved one are seeking a more energetic, uplifting, socially active experience or a shared intense "insight" adventure, you'll want to use high-THC cannabis products, which generally are those made from sativa strains.

Much of the labeling on legally marketed cannabis products can be misleading. Try to find a local dispensary or dealer you can trust to provide you with a high-THC, low-CBD cannabis product, and sample several different ones until you find one that you and your partner prefer.

Research is beginning to suggest that a number of the minor chemicals found in the cannabis flower are subtle but important for a maximum high. Unfortunately, most of these constituents are removed in the process of distilling cannabis for use in edibles, oils, and other refined products. For this reason, the traditional method of smoking the full-bud mixture in a pipe, cigarette, or water pipe, rather than ingesting a refined product, is often the best plan. More on that later.

PREDICTABLE EFFECTS

Considering that cannabis research has been legally challenging in the past and today is still in its infancy, what do we actually know about the plant's effects?[14] To begin, on a physical level, well-verified medical research shows that when you smoke marijuana with a moderate THC level, initially your pulse will tend to quicken and your blood pressure might rise a bit (or a lot, if the marijuana has a high THC content) before dropping back down to normal. Your body temperature will drop slightly, and your breathing will usually deepen. Often you'll feel whole-body muscular relaxation within minutes of smoking. All of these effects also occur when you ingest a refined cannabis product, but more slowly, usually manifesting within an hour.

Marijuana's effects are said to be 50 percent chemical and 50 percent psychological – your mood, expectation, personality type, cognitive habits, and other variables strongly influence how your brain and body respond to the chemicals. The overall psychological effect for most people includes relaxation, contentment, sensory pleasure, a shift in mind-set into present-moment sensory or fantasy focus, an altered sense of the flow of time (a sense of timelessness), slight euphoria, and general sense of well-being.

Marijuana is often called an insight drug – it has the power to elicit deep new experience and insight, especially when approached mindfully.

High-THC cannabis is considered to be psychotropic, which means that it noticeably affects your mind and inner subjective experience and causes changes in mental and emotional functioning. In the past, cannabis was traditionally included in the group of psychotropes known as hallucinogens, but most researchers now agree that marijuana very seldom induces a full-blown psychedelic experience – but high doses can indeed lead to hallucinatory audio and visual alterations and other intense inner experiences.[15]

Rarely, but of import, a few users sometimes experience temporary anxiety and even panic when they first try cannabis, probably as a result of the sudden loss of ego control of their inner experience.[16] This shift from habitual mental control of our inner experience into a freer, participatory experience of spontaneous engagement in the moment is, of course, what most of us are seeking when we get high. But for first-time smokers, that effect can be surprising and may trigger anxiety.

A lot of baby boomers whom I've worked with had this initial "freak-out" experience when they first tried grass long ago, often in a negative social setting, and they never tried it again. I hope that the suggestions throughout this book and in the High Together app will help those of you with this history to approach the experience of getting high in a confident, enjoyable way. Remember that as a general rule, it's easier to get too much THC when you eat, drink, or dab a cannabis product. This is another reason to smoke rather than ingest marijuana; smoking allows you to regulate your intake and experiment, puff by puff, to find your right strain and dosage.

It's true that eating or drinking a marijuana product can generate somewhat similar effects as smoking weed, but there are notable differences: the onset is much slower when you eat or drink it, and the psychological impact is somewhat different and more subtle.

When you eat cannabis, the THC goes first to your liver, where, as recent studies have shown, the chemical is broken down into a metabolite called 11-hydroxy-THC.[17] To date, there has been almost no research on this metabolite, so we really don't know much about how it affects the body and brain.

Many people who enjoy smoking grass do not like eating it because ingestion tends to make them feel heavy rather than light and sluggish rather than energized. The mental stimulation, erogenous glow, and shared sense of insight and discovery tend to be dulled when you ingest rather than smoke the herb. But, of course, a lot of people eat and fly high – it's your choice.

NATURAL RECEPTORS

In the late 1960s, Dr. Raphael Mechoulam, an Israeli scientist, first isolated and identified the chief cannabinoid, THC.[18] The pure compound was then synthesized, making exact pharmacological studies and products possible. Twenty years later, a team of American researchers, led by neurobiologist Allyn Howlett, identified THC-sensitive receptor sites in human brain cells.[19]

Those receptors, known as cannabinoid receptors, bind with anandamide, an endogenous (made by the body) chemical that generates effects quite similar to those provoked by THC. As it turns out, the THC molecule is so similar to the anandamide molecule that it is capable of binding to those same receptors. This, then, is the mechanism by which THC triggers a neurobiological response. Cannabinoid receptors are widely distributed in the brain and also everywhere in the central nervous system, which means that THC can readily bind to sites around your entire body, not just in your brain.[20]

The chemistry is remarkably complex and still not fully understood, but we do know that the natural cannabinoids produced by the body – the endocannabinoids, as they're known – modulate a large number of physiological processes related to pain, memory, movement, muscle tone, sleep, pleasure, and appetite.

When inhaled (such as when you smoke cannabis), THC and other active cannabis constituents are absorbed rapidly (within three seconds) through the respiratory tract and lungs into the bloodstream, generating an onset of effects in the brain in just a few minutes. With the new hyper-strong buds, most people need only two or three inhalations to move into the "stimulating" first phase of the marijuana experience.

This initial temporary "rush" can feel so intense that you won't want to even consider driving or any physical activity for fifteen to twenty minutes; it's best to just kick back and enjoy the experience. The intensity subsides gradually after thirty to sixty minutes, and for most people and most doses the high ends after two to three hours. Subtle effects, such as a feeling of relaxation, may linger for several more hours or even into the next day. Indeed, considerable amounts of THC stay in your bloodstream for several days afterward.

When you eat or drink cannabis, your body absorbs the THC

through your digestive tract and much more slowly, with blood con-centrations increasing steadily for three or more hours.[21] You typically won't feel any effects until at least half an hour, and up to two hours, after consumption.[22] Rather than a sudden euphoric effect, the initial impact of eating cannabis is usually a gradual, pleasant slowing-down feeling in the body, a sedate and calm shifting of gears in the mind, and often a much-valued reduction in pain and bodily sensations of all kinds.

A gender note: A careful review of research published in a report on marijuana that was prepared for the Canadian Senate concluded that there are no observable differences in the metabolic effect of cannabis on men and women. Both male and female subjects alike report a sudden shift into an altered state of awareness – and it's exactly this particular cognitive and perceptual shift and the resulting inner experiences that users value so highly.

THE EXPERIENCE

Let's look a bit more deeply into reports describing the shift into the marijuana mind-set.[23] At first, especially if you have smoked or vaped cannabis, you will likely feel a sudden unique quality of mild pleasure or even euphoria occurring throughout your body. Your breathing rate and the depth of your inhalations and exhalations change – usually in the direction of more relaxed, deep, and calm, and there predictably ensues a sudden shift in the quality and content of your consciousness.

As the THC takes effect, the ego's habitual control over what you do and feel and think will temporarily let go, and your focus will shift spontaneously from busy past-future thoughts and plans into a present-moment sense of liberation from your mind's usual mental fixations.

At the same time, an enjoyable physical relaxation usually takes over your muscles, along with definite and often quite interesting perceptual alterations. For instance, your sense of the flow of time may shift. Time may seem to expand, and a few minutes can seem like an hour – many people report getting "much more experience out of a minute" than usual. (This is perhaps a primary desired effect of the drug, and we'll explore it experientially in later chapters.)

Also, you'll probably feel a heightening of sensory alertness and bodily pleasure as a fresh, early-childhood type of raw perception takes over – everything you look at or hear or touch suddenly seems new, interesting, and aesthetically pleasing.[24] In a word, marijuana tends to help us see the world through more creative and nonjudgmental eyes.

This expanded sense of time, pleasure, and focus may be accompanied by auditory experiences, such as hearing music or other ambient sounds. Especially when closing the eyes, some people also report mild hallucinatory images, where a pleasurable inner light show, fantasy, or imaginary reality temporarily fills the mind's inner screen.[25]

Many marijuana users also report a sudden, quite pleasurable intensification of ordinary sensory experiences such as eating, watching TV, conversation, listening to birds singing, swimming, dancing, walking in nature, and making love.

In a social setting, marijuana is well known for provoking infectious laughter and a humorous perspective on life. The positive energetic discharge that accompanies whole-body laughter is one of the main features of getting high. Even the basic act of conversing with another person, face-to-face, can become intense and especially meaningful, even quite intimate. Especially when you also drink alcohol, your inhibitions can drop away, and socialization becomes more highly charged, and you may feel inspired with bright new ideas.[26] (Note: While it's been proven that consuming one or two alcoholic drinks before taking weed will boost the impact of the weed in your system, drinking more than that will most likely impair your system and prevent you from being present for any meaningful relating.)

In all honesty, most people tend to use marijuana because it makes them feel good. This is one of the reasons it's so effective in reducing pain and other forms of suffering – it boosts our overall enjoyment of life. And because it has so few negative side effects, marijuana is fast becoming an effective medical treatment as well as a recreational mood booster.

All these altered experiences come together to generate a special sense of shared interaction when you get high with a close friend. In the chapters that follow, we're going to look more deeply into how each of the seven typical dimensions of a shared high can be guided and augmented in order to maximize the intimate event you're moving through.

MENTAL PERFORMANCE

A search for scientific information on the cognitive effects of cannabis can seem dismal – you'll find a lot of negatives and almost no positives. As Dr. Sanjay Gupta points out, "About 6 percent of the current U.S. marijuana studies investigate the benefits of medical marijuana. The rest are designed to investigate harm. That imbalance paints a highly distorted picture." He further points out that while someone dies every nineteen minutes from prescription drug overdose, there are no records of even a single death from marijuana overdose.[27]

That said, here's what we can conclude fairly definitively: Getting high definitely has some trade-offs. On a temporary basis, marijuana intake will affect both your mental and your physical abilities.

To begin, research shows that a person who has taken pot will experience pronounced (but temporary) cognitive alterations.[28] Sometimes it will cause you to have deficits in your short-term memory ("What was I just doing?"). However, in exchange, your inner experience will expand, and you may move through a pleasurable free flow of associations. Freed from your usual inhibitions and conditioned beliefs, you can find yourself entertaining fresh thoughts and seeing the world from a unique and brighter perspective.

New ideas and insights will come effortlessly to mind, allowing you to shift into unexpected thought flows, pleasing reveries, and vivid fantasy adventures. The experience of your imagination will seem more real and engaging, combining with your expanded perceptions to stimulate a whole new universe of inner experience.

In the first thirty minutes to two hours after you've smoked marijuana, when your mind is engaged in just "being," formal studies show that your motor skills and reaction times are indeed temporarily slowed down, and skilled activity can be negatively affected. Marijuana is definitely a drug, and it does at times generate serious alterations that can be both bothersome and outright dangerous if not approached mindfully. So when using pot, you'll probably want to temporarily put aside your daily routines, refrain from driving, and shift from "doing" to "being" for an hour or two, just relaxing into the experience that comes to you.

As noted before, each person responds to the effects of THC in their own unique way depending on their personality, social situation, mood, energy level, and so forth. Your experience will not be the same as anyone else's; it may not even be the same between sessions.

Within the general parameters of the marijuana high, each time you choose to smoke, dab, or ingest cannabis, an utterly unexpected experience can emerge. When you ingest coffee or alcohol – or morphine or cocaine, for that matter – you can be fairly sure about how you're going to react because our reactions to these substances are fairly predictable. With marijuana, however, you must be ready for a wide variety of possible physical and mental reaction. This is one of the complex attributes of cannabis.

When you partake of the herb with your friend as a shared adventure, it's important to remember that your friend/partner will not have the exact same experience as you. Even when you're sharing an idea and speaking similar words, in reality your inner experience won't be fully congruent with your partner's. As you move through a number of shared experiences, you'll develop a growing appreciation for the fact that you're actually always alone with your inner experience, even while communicating about it.

One of the beautiful paradoxes of sharing a high session is that you can feel so totally in tune with your friend, even while remaining aware that you're having different experiences.

Regarding whether marijuana negatively affects your memory, wildly conflicting scientific reports abound. Reliable cognitive studies have shown that marijuana use temporarily impairs, or at least alters, short-term memory. But these studies are very general, and none of them to date (that I know of) have explored whether you can train yourself to maintain a sharp memory while you are high. Also, a 2018 study conducted at the University of Florida found that cannabis actually seems to improve memory – so go figure.[29]

When they first experiment with grass, many people find that they are unable to make their mind function "normally" when they are high, and they find this upsetting. As I said before, there's a definite trade-off happening here – in the same way that you wouldn't drink a six-pack and then do your taxes, you probably wouldn't want to smoke a strong strain of grass and then attend a corporate strategy meeting – unless you know that you perform well at that level when you are high. Anecdotally, many people find that they can train themselves to perform well at desired tasks when they are high – it's largely a matter of focus, practice, and intent.

In order to safely and securely enjoy the benefits of marijuana, most people need to set time aside, relax their normal mental

habits, and gracefully surrender temporary short-term
memory functions in exchange for unique and
powerful shifts in awareness.

AVOIDING DOWNSIDES

Although cannabis has been well documented as being quite benign in its effects, it's true that it can cause a small percentage of first-time users to slip temporarily into anxiety. When I worked with a team of researchers at Princeton University to study college students using cannabis, we found that about 10 percent of first-time users reacted with a short anxiety/panic attack.[30]

My own first marijuana experience (a very strong dose of pure hashish) began with a sudden ten-minute anxiety attack because I started imagining the police busting in and catching me in the act of something totally illegal and also widely condemned as immoral. I also was afraid that using marijuana might make me go crazy – permanently. A friend who was in the room saw my reaction, came over to where I was sitting, and calmly took my hand, met my eyes, and smiled – and in just a few breaths I started to feel okay again.

Surveys have documented that a surprising number of everyday Americans have a mostly buried fear that taking a drug that pushes them into an altered state of consciousness will cause them to become crazy. Early antimarijuana propaganda played upon this fear, actively pushing the idea that pot use could induce a sudden psychotic break or even permanent mental illness.[31]

> Even with loads of proof to the contrary, many people are
> fearful that they might go crazy or do something bad or
> harmful if they surrender their habitual ego control,
> even once, to a psychotropic drug.

Is this in any way a valid fear? Studies show that very large doses of pure THC sometimes produce symptoms of temporary psychosis in rigid personality types or in unstable personalities that are genetically prone to schizophrenia.[32] Symptoms such as confusion, amnesia, delusions, hallucinations, anxiety, and agitation do sometimes emerge when a person is under the influence of pot – especially if the environment becomes threatening or confusing. The same thing often happens with an overdose of alcohol.

THC-intensive cannabis can temporarily induce some of the more benign symptoms of schizophrenia, in which time stretches out, colors become more vivid, and mental fantasies manifest as visual images. In fact, many people seek out and fully enjoy these altered states.

Other so-called "psychotic" experiences are also occasionally part of the overall marijuana high, especially with large doses. These include temporary difficulty in making decisions, trouble focusing or paying attention, problems with working memory, sensory distortions, unusual thoughts, and quite vivid fantasies. For most people, these symptoms are short-lived (lasting a few minutes or so) and often quite pleasurable and insightful. Only in extreme cases or when eating very large doses of THC do such symptoms persist for longer than half an hour, and they do not continue after the effects of the drug have worn off.

> The current mainstream psychiatric opinion in the United States is that cannabis on its own does not cause schizophrenia or other psychiatric disorders and it is a fairly safe drug in regard to mental health.

The inner experience of temporarily letting go of ego control and trusting the flow of the marijuana experience is almost always a good feeling, a positive learning experience, and a liberating, insightful, and predictably healthy adventure. More and more people now use marijuana recreationally with this clear intent of temporarily "getting out of their mind" and relaxing into a more laid-back, spontaneous, enjoyable marijuana high.

In sum: Everyone has his or her own unique experience with the herb, and the experience is usually very enjoyable. Using marijuana is always an adventure to be approached with respect and a bit of mindful caution – but with no need for worry.

PHYSICAL HEALTH

Is marijuana entirely benign in terms of its effect on our physical health? Current research indicates that moderate smoking of cannabis poses minimal danger to the lungs, although heavy daily smoking might possibly lead to complications. Unlike heavy tobacco smokers, most heavy cannabis smokers exhibit no obstruction of the lung's small airways, indicating that most people won't develop emphysema from smoking cannabis.

Australian studies show that people who smoke cannabis throughout the day for years on end but don't smoke tobacco are only slightly more likely than nonsmokers to make outpatient visits for respiratory illnesses.

Similar studies that adjust for sex, age, race, education, and alcohol consumption suggest that daily cannabis smokers have a slightly elevated risk of respiratory illness compared to nonsmokers. But curiously, studies of cannabis smokers in New Zealand and at UCLA found that smoking cannabis on a daily basis for an average of twenty years actually led to a lower prevalence of emphysema and asthma than in the general population.[33] And THC itself doesn't appear to be carcinogenic.

The *Cannabis Report* released in 1999 by the Swiss Federal Commission for Drug Issues (EKDF) concluded that cannabis is probably the most widely smoked substance in the world after tobacco, and its main adverse effect is its definite negative effect on psychomotor performance. Cannabis, the report concluded, usually (but not always) slows your reaction time and interferes with your muscle control, thereby impairing your ability to drive a car, play sports, or perform any activity that requires coordination or strength.[34]

As predicted, studies have documented that THC can produce dose-related impairments in a wide range of cognitive and behavioral functions relevant to skilled performance, such as operating machinery. These impairments include slightly slowed reaction time; lax information processing; impaired perceptual-motor coordination and performance; weak short-term memory, attention, signal detection, and tracking behavior; and distorted time perception.[35]

A number of related reports conclude that cannabis can impair performance in simulated driving settings, but studies of the effects of cannabis on actual on-the-road driving performance have thus far found only slight impairments.[36] People who are cannabis-intoxicated (by a very high dose) tend to drive more slowly and cautiously, whereas people who are alcohol-intoxicated generally drive at faster-than-normal speeds and take more risks. But of course, the mix of alcohol and pot can produce very nasty effects for anyone who is driving.

In our media, hardly a week goes by without some magazine or newspaper carrying a questionable story about marijuana, that "dangerous drug," shrinking the amygdala, rewiring the brain, or otherwise destroying young minds. This often unfounded reporting makes everybody afraid of pot, even as more serious research shows that in most cases it isn't doing any noticeable damage at all. Using functional magnetic resonance imaging (fMRI) technologies, researchers at several universities have now reversed a number of earlier studies and found almost no evidence of brain damage in people who enjoy regular high times with cannabis. Brain-wave patterns of chronic cannabis users versus those of non-users show zero differentiation, even though cannabis definitely lights up an fMRI scan in unique ways for a person who is high.

In fact, cannabis may actually have neuroprotective qualities. Professor Yosef Sarne of Tel Aviv University's Sackler Faculty of Medicine documented that low doses of THC protect the brain from long-term cognitive damage after injury due to hypoxia, toxic drugs, or seizure. He showed that low doses have a positive impact on cell signaling, preventing cell death and promoting growth factors. Sarne's current research indicates that low doses of THC may also prevent damage to the heart caused by cardiac ischemia.[37]

In sum: From the best research I can find to date, it appears
that even long-term heavy use of cannabis by adults produces
no evidence of debilitating impairment of cognitive function
when users are not high.

SENSATION BOOST

Does marijuana give people the munchies? Will you get fat if you
smoke pot? I would have to say that it depends. If your self-control is
weak and you keep too many snacks readily available, you are indeed
at risk of overeating (though, of course, that's true whether or not you
are using marijuana). However, a 2013 study found that Americans
who smoke pot actually have smaller waists than people who don't.
So who's to say?

Regarding the munchies, it's true. In one study, college-age subjects smoked either a placebo or active cannabis twice a day. Those
subjects who smoked active cannabis increased their food intake – and
doubled their snack consumption – during both private and social
periods, with the greatest rate of change in caloric intake occurring in
social settings.

In fact, many people smoke cannabis regularly *because* it improves
their appetite. Otherwise, for various medical reasons, they wouldn't eat
properly or enough. So yes, cannabis does increase our appetite for food,
just as it often increases our appetite for visual stimulation, music, and
physical pleasures, such as sex.

Evidence shows that grass can intensify pleasurable sensations
of all kinds. It can, in a word, serve as an aphrodisiac,
ranging from moderate to extreme, for any of the
senses or all of them at once.

Marijuana makes everyday pleasures more pleasurable, and as various studies have documented, the key to understanding this temporary
enhancement of pleasure lies in the way that marijuana intensifies our

focus of attention toward a unique mix of present-moment experience, imagination, and memory. Our power to guide our marijuana experience lies in our ongoing choice of where we focus our attention. If we focus on food, we'll probably eat. If we focus on springtime flowers, we'll enjoy that rush of visual pleasure. If we focus on the physical presence of our loved one, sexual pleasures will perhaps arise. We'll explore in later chapters how to manage our focal choices in order to generate the experiences we want to have when we are high.

OTHER WORRIES?

Obviously, if cannabis could be proven to be detrimental to any aspect of our lives, opponents to pot legalization would have presented their case loud and clear. In fact, cannabis used in moderation doesn't create serious health concerns for most people, and from what we currently know, it has a positive impact on many mood disorders.

However, for the 10 to 15 percent of our population who are already at high risk of mental problems (such as borderline schizophrenia or latent psychosis), marijuana can provoke an outbreak of these conditions. It is wise to be aware of this possibility. Also, even if you're fairly stable emotionally, be careful not to overdose on the edibles, as that is what causes most panic attacks.

Hold in mind that psychological studies show that if people have a panic attack caused by their first experience with cannabis, they usually have just one. If you have one, don't be afraid that it will happen again.

Note: If you or a partner have a panic attack or any other upsetting reaction to getting high, before rushing off to the emergency room, I recommend following the steps outlined in "8 Ways to Counteract a Too-Intense Cannabis High," which you can find on the Leafly website. Usually a cannabis-induced panic attack will dissipate in five to ten minutes.

To make sure that you're not caught up in worrying when you use marijuana, let's look at some other media-provoked worries, most of which have been proven invalid. For instance, do people get addicted to pot? A review of the research shows that the answer is almost never, especially if by "addicted" you mean physiologically dependent, as with alcohol, amphetamines, tobacco, opiates, and many prescription drugs, where withdrawal from the substance is extreme.[38]

However, abrupt withdrawal from marijuana following very heavy daily use has been shown to sometimes cause temporary withdrawal symptoms such as irritability, nausea, perspiration, trembling, insomnia, and loss of appetite. These withdrawal symptoms are relatively minor and short in duration, lasting usually just a day or two.[39]

> Psychologically, any substance taken regularly to induce a positive inner experience or to escape from negative emotions will generate psychological dependence, especially if the person is using the drug to avoid painful inner experience and neurotic emotional patterns.

We're all dependent on a variety of substances and experiences that we've become habitually fond of ingesting or receiving – and we resist the loss of these things or experiences. We love our comfort zones! But beyond everyday habits that we're attached to, some of us are more prone to acute states of habituation than others, based on our genes, childhood, and physiology.

Several decades ago, a colleague of mine in New York conducted a landmark study for the National Institutes of Health (NIH) related to heroin use. He found that about 20 percent of America's adult population seems to have a strong addictive tendency related to the drug – their body, not just their mind, craves the drug at cellular levels.

However, if given ready access to heroin, about 50 percent of the population might use it now and then recreationally but would not become physically addicted; in other words, they can take it or leave it. Another 25 percent will become nauseous upon taking heroin – they cannot tolerate the drug. A recent government report states: "The genes a person is born with account for about half of that person's risk for addiction. Gender, ethnicity, and the presence of other mental disorders also influence risk of addiction."[40] I mention this information just to clear up a common misconception that anyone using cocaine or heroin will immediately become addicted. Marijuana is not physically addictive.

In sum, concern about addiction to marijuana is not an issue for most people, although psychological dependency is always possible when marijuana is being used to avoid the need for emotional growth.

If you want to keep up on the science of cannabis, you can easily monitor the research online, but we're still years away from getting all the necessary research funded and completed. For our *Cannabis for Couples* theme, where a moderate dose of cannabis is taken no more than once a day, the evidence is quite strong that you have nothing to fear and loads to look forward to. Check our website for postings of important new updates.

As a final note, a recent personality-type study using the Myers-Briggs questionnaire has dismissed the media stereotype that marijuana users tend to be introverted, withdrawn, passive, quiet, lazy, and shy. Quite the contrary. The study, in which more than two thousand marijuana users were interviewed, found that the dominant personality type among them was extroverted, not introverted. In the general population, 50 percent of people score as extroverted; among the marijuana users, that number was 80 percent.

Contrary to the stoner stereotype, the majority of cannabis users enjoy interacting with people, maintain a wide circle of acquaintances, and gain energy from social situations. They tend to be social by nature and are often charming and witty. They tend to be creative, resourceful, spontaneous, and impulsive. Rather than being withdrawn and quiet, they are outgoing risk takers who are curious about almost everything. And they want their relationships to be full of excitement and adventure. So . . . another stereotype bites the dust, and the personality of cannabis users shifts in our minds.

THREE

Couples Choosing Cannabis

As you tap into the marijuana muse
and discover your personal power
to manifest your vision,
remember that your ego
is not the ultimate source
of your vision and power –
you are tapped into the all.

What makes one couple choose to include cannabis in their life, while another couple decides not to? And how do two people reach the point where they actually act on their decision to include cannabis in their intimate relating?

In this chapter we're going to follow three quite different couples as they move through the decision-making process that enables both members of the dyad to feel comfortable about experimenting together with marijuana. We'll also present a set of questions that will help you reflect with your partner about seven key issues related to your decision, and we include evaluation questions for you to review if you're already using cannabis together.

Note on gender: Our society is evolving rapidly beyond the stereotype of a heterosexual couple to the point that we now include the full spectrum of sexual identities and preferences. I'm going to feature in this chapter three couples who represent the large majority of couples in our society, but this in no way means that I'm not fully cognizant and openly supportive of all variations on the sexual-identity theme.

As documented in current surveys, most Americans assume that around 20 percent of our population is homosexual or bisexual. I myself was surprised to find that the actual percentages are quite different. Only 1.3 percent of women and 1.9 percent of men under the age of forty report being gay, with an added 5.5 percent of women and 2 percent of men identifying as bisexual. About 17.4 percent of women report having had at least one same-sex experience, while 6.2 percent of straight men report that they have had at least one gay encounter. In sum, American gay and bisexual individuals together total 4.5 percent of our population.[1]

Whether you're gay, straight, or anything in between, the discussions in this book will work equally well. As I'm by inclination fairly straight, please forgive me if I make any assumptions that don't fully fit your sexual orientation, preference, and experience. The spirit of this book is to be inclusive throughout.

The three couples I'd like to introduce you to, drawn from friends and clients over the years, represent our three main population groups: young couples exploring their first months and years together before perhaps having children; middle-aged couples who are perhaps integrating intimate relating and child-rearing; and retired or soon-to-retire couples whose kids (if any) have flown the coop, opening up a new, hopefully more relaxed phase of life.

I have changed the names and biographical notes on these three couples, as is usual in a book like this, but their experiences still ring genuine and represent a great many of us exploring intimacy with cannabis. You will, of course, most likely focus on the couple representing your age group and situation, but do also listen to the other two couples, as their perspectives are quite insightful for all of us. And of course, you might find that your own situation falls somewhere between these examples.

YOUNG AND EXPLORING

Our first couple came to me for cannabis-unrelated reasons – they were struggling to gracefully break free from one of their fathers, who was being overly domineering in their lives. In this context, and in the friendship that developed between us over the next year or so, I learned of their interest but uncertainty regarding marijuana. Jennifer had gotten high a few times with an earlier boyfriend in college, but Terry had come from a conservative religious family and thus far had avoided any contact with cannabis.

"My parents considered marijuana to be of the devil," he told me. "They also thought that Jenn was too wild to make a serious mate for me, but they're beginning to warm to her, step by step. And it's true, she's helped me to stop being so bashful, to open up, and to be more spontaneous."

"Well," Jenn said with a smile, sitting comfortably beside him on the couch across from me, "I'm more of an extrovert. I've always rushed into things without much forethought. That's how I ended up getting high in college. It was just something that was going around, and it seemed harmless enough."

Terry shifted his position, seeming uncomfortable. "My dad would've shot me if he found out I smoked pot."

"I actually liked it," Jenn offered. "It helped me relax and enjoy, well, everything. But it also showed me that the guy I was with was too self-centered. He got stoned and just went off inward somewhere. I guess my first insights with grass were all about realizing that I was with the wrong person."

Terry turned toward her, uncertain. "What if we smoke that stuff and you realize the same thing about me?" He was a little choked up.

She grinned at him impishly. "Oh, I've checked that out already," she said. "I married you, not him. And that's why I want you to talk with John about this. You know in general I don't like drugs, and not even much alcohol, but I still remember getting high and feeling like my mind opened up, and my heart too. Is it wrong that I want to have that experience with you? And hey, I felt closer to God when I was high than when I wasn't. Is that a sin?"

He looked at her seriously for a moment. I could tell he was a good-hearted guy who really loved his wife. "I just question whether using a drug can ever be a positive thing in a relationship," he told her. Then he looked at me. "From my background, people like you should be locked up. You're pushing drugs, and that's bad. I mean, that's what my father would say."

"And you?" I asked him evenly.

"Oh, that's obvious, isn't it? I trust Jenn. She's helped me wake up to so much. I mean, she's got me meditating, and we do that together, and it's just getting more and more deep and interesting for me. But drugs?"

"I came from a similar background," I told him. "It took me a while to realize that marijuana is its own unique thing, and yes, I do find it a positive additive in my own life. It has a special power to open our hearts. But I also respect your hesitation. Grass is potent, and it needs to be approached wisely if you decide to try it."

"I guess what scares me really is the whole idea of losing control, of letting some chemical take me over," he confessed.

"But that's the whole point," Jenn interjected. "Especially with religious stuff, we're supposed to keep a tight rein on our impulses and never lose control, but hey, what about trusting your natural instincts?

When I got high, that's what I discovered – that I didn't have to be afraid of my own self. I mean, you love me, all of me, right? Are you afraid I'm going to turn into the devil when we get high?"

He laughed. "Well, I was brought up afraid that the devil was always out there, lurking in the shadows, ready to tempt me into sin if I didn't keep my guard up."

"And you still believe that?" she pushed him.

"Hmm. Not really. And I'm open to experimenting a little. Maybe I'm afraid I'll embarrass myself if I get high and lose control."

"Well, that's a valid concern," I told him. "And you shouldn't feel any pressure to try pot. You're just fine as you are. But there's also the possibility that the two of you might open up and have some valuable experiences together if you get high."

He let a slight smile light up his face. "Maybe I'm just afraid to have fun," he admitted. "My parents never cut loose ever, you know. And I admit, I sometimes feel like I'm in a straitjacket, even in bed with Jenn."

"Maybe some structure would help," I offered. "It might be wise to approach taking cannabis in ways that help you feel safe and secure."

"Hey, I'm open to new things. I mean, every day with Jenn seems to bring something new that I really like. So . . . what are you suggesting?"

I gave him a brief outline of what we're exploring in this book, and then our session was over. When I talked with them again, two weeks later, Terry had this to say: "Oh, I was being really defensive about the whole thing. I mean it's true – that stuff is very interesting and strong and not to be messed with. But the experience itself wasn't at all what I expected: just the opposite. I didn't feel pushed into anything."

"We used that little water pipe you recommended," Jenn mentioned, "and the smoke didn't hardly burn our lungs at all, not like the joints I used to smoke."

"Being in our apartment, safe and alone together, helped too,"

Terry said. "I was nervous, sure. It felt like when we were in Hawaii and I did a bungee jump – that same scary feeling. But then all of a sudden, just a few minutes in, things just, well, it all just flowed, like there wasn't any scary stuff at all. I was just suddenly flowing into this new place, with a new feeling in my body, and hey, I admit, we had such a time!"

PARENTAL HIGH

In America today, almost 50 percent of married couples don't have children. For couples who do have children, the cannabis decision is a bit complex. Lots of couples who used cannabis together early in their relationship tend to stop smoking when they have their first child.

My wife and I mostly put cannabis aside when our first child arrived, except for the occasional weekend puff. We were busy, we were happy, and our circle of friends centered around the parents in our children's school – and most of them looked down on marijuana, especially in the family setting.

Let's look at this more closely. First, is it, in fact, bad to use cannabis when you are pregnant or nursing?

As I'm writing this book, the research remains seriously inadequate. Studies have shown that THC does cross the placental barrier and enter the fetal bloodstream. Several studies with rats show that a very high continuous dosage of THC in the mother can possibly cause alterations in brain development in the fetus. But we simply don't yet have enough evidence to make a definitive statement.[2]

This is unfortunate because marijuana has proven to be of great help in relieving morning sickness in the first three months of pregnancy – but this is also the key time for brain development in the fetus. So many pregnant women choose to follow the "precautionary principle" of abstaining during pregnancy and while nursing. I advise you to stay up to date regarding new research that might help you decide whether to use cannabis if you're pregnant or considering pregnancy.

The most up-to-date study I could find took place with 600,000 pregnant women in Canada. The study's authors found that women who smoked cannabis regularly while pregnant had a slight tendency toward a premature birth. However, that difference could possibly be explained by the fact that 58 percent of the cannabis-using mothers smoked cigarettes versus only 8 percent of the non-users, and tobacco use also increases the risk of prematurity. The cannabis-using mothers were also relatively underweight compared with the non-users.

The good news is that even with its large sample size, the study revealed no startling or upsetting statistics. Perhaps cannabis use during pregnancy causes a slightly increased risk of premature birth, but that increase (3 percent) was barely significant statistically. I can find no studies evaluating brain-wave function in infants whose mothers used cannabis during their pregnancy, but based on the positive Israeli studies of cannabis improving general neural health, it's possible that smoking pot while pregnant could improve your baby's health profile, rather than detracting from it. With such a small difference in the effect between using and not using, my best advice would be that you should follow your heart and do what feels right – but do keep abreast of new research.

Moderation is a good choice for parents using marijuana. Smoking marijuana in small dosages now and then will probably cause no harm. But heavy use of cannabis, especially for a woman who is pregnant or breastfeeding, seems, well, extreme – and a definite risk to avoid.

Another key question for parents is this: Can we be good parents and be high at the same time?

Having little kids means assuming full responsibility for them. Can we do that while high? That's a challenging question with no definitive answer. Certainly, caring for very young children while high can be difficult. Marijuana can shift our focus of attention in ways that may temporarily take our attention away from our child – and this can be dangerous, of course. Also, for some parents, being high can cause a temporary state of spaced-out introversion and self-absorption, depriving the child of focused, loving attention that he or she may need in the moment.

I don't want to dictate your decision on this issue, but at the same time, I think we need open discussion of this topic in our society as more and more parents do start using marijuana. There are dangers to be guarded against, but as with many things, the issue is dependent on many factors. You often see not-high parents being rather distant from their youngster, distracted by adult thoughts and activities rather than paying attention to the child. And I've observed parents who, when high, become more attuned to the present moment, and thus more attentive and loving to their child and a better parent during that time. So it can go both ways.

In general, based on my own observations (and not any formal research), I'd say that parents of young children seem to do better caring for their child when they are not high.

You'll have to decide what's best for your children, honestly considering your own unique response to getting high, and holding in mind that your response can change over time and with many factors. Regardless, when your children are at school or when they're asleep, you can definitely find time, perhaps once or twice a week, to take a few hours off and indulge in a deep, intimate cannabis-touched retreat.

I remember the parents of a boy in our son's school who were struggling with this question. The father, Greg, worked in construction at the time, and he liked to come home at night, take a few puffs, and relax. His son seemed to enjoy spending time with him when Greg was in a high state. It's easy to get high and loll around the living room or yard and goof off with a child – everybody seems to like that.

But Greg's wife, Annette, had made herself a solemn vow that when she got pregnant, she'd stop smoking grass altogether. One weekend my wife and I were at a school picnic with Greg and Annette, and the topic arose between the four of us. "I just don't go into that party mode anymore," she said. "Being a parent means letting go of partying. And really, I don't miss it. I remember how Greg and I used to get really high and tipsy, and it wasn't very deep between us back then."

"Well, I still like it," Greg said. "Not the partying so much, but hey, we had our good times back then."

"Times change," she concluded. "I need a clear head these days. And when you get high around the house, you often drift off on your own and leave me to take care of little Jack."

"Do I?"

"Ummm . . . yep. Sometimes."

"Well, you go off and meditate before coming to bed. That's about the same thing. Maybe I miss getting high with you."

They sat there staring at each other. "Maybe there's a third alternative," I put in.

"Yes?"

"You could set aside a couple of hours when the two of you can be all alone, and hang out, and just see what happens if you get high with the intent to focus on each other. You also might agree to follow a bit of structure to help you stay present and relate rather than drifting off."

"Hmm," from both of them, tentatively.

"Marijuana tends to give us what we choose to focus on," I added, not wanting to push too much into their intimate life. "If you're content with how things are, fine. But if you'd both like to enjoy something new together, you might see what happens if you set up a bit of a shared process to follow when you get high together, after Jackie's asleep or at school. If you haven't gotten high together for a few years, it will definitely be a new experience – an adventure to share."

"Hmm," from Greg.

"The thing about getting high," I went on, "is that the sky's the limit when it comes to what two people can discover about each other, and what you can discover about your own self."

My words hung a bit in the air. They finally turned and looked into each other's eyes. Then they both smiled slightly to each other. "Well, maybe that does interest me," she said.

"Sounds a bit intense," he said.

"Come on, I know you like intense," she shot back at him, but with an intimate undertone.

"Well, for me weed isn't some deep thing," he said. "It's just for fun. It shifts me out of work gear, that's all. It's not like your meditation. In fact, it's just the opposite."

"A lot of people get high and meditate," I offered. "It all depends on your intent. Change the intent and a new experience can happen. That's what I've found – if you get high and are open to something new, that's probably what you'll get."

"Maybe I'd like that," she said.

"But what about your no-pot vows?" he countered. "Aren't you afraid you won't be a good mom anymore?"

Again they looked into each other's eyes. "Well, once a week won't hurt anything," she decided. "And I do feel left out sometimes when you smoke and then go giggle with Jackie and I don't. I'm open to once a week. And Thursdays are open."

"But I wouldn't know what to do," he said hesitantly. "Maybe I'd just space out like usual."

"I can suggest a few things to help with that," I offered, and I proceeded to share with them some tips for staying tuned in to each other and not slipping off into the ozone.

A week later, Greg phoned me. He had some questions and also a report: Things had gone well. They were going to do it again next week. In fact, they'd set up two nights a week to get high together and continue with their exploration. I was pleased. There's never really any way to know what's going to happen in such a situation until a couple tries it and they find out for themselves.

RETIRED . . . BUT STILL OPEN

In many ways, marijuana seems to have been made for life after retirement. After all, you no longer have children whom you're responsible for every day; you don't have to spend your time, attention, and energy on your career; hopefully you're still in good health and mentally bright. You have at least a decade or two ahead of you to do just whatever you want to. More and more states won't bother you with laws about cannabis intake – and most of the ones that still outlaw recreational use will let you use cannabis for all sorts of medical reasons and excuses. What a golden opportunity!

On the other hand, if you've been conditioned all your life to consider cannabis a bad drug that will destroy your life, you'll still tend to reject the very notion of getting high as a bright, positive thing to do with your loved one.

Attitudes about recreational drug use are ingrained and often quite difficult to move beyond. And really, in the final active phase of your life, why should you do anything so risky as experiment with a consciousness-altering drug?

Again, I'm not here to try to convince anyone to use marijuana. If you're not attracted to the idea, that's perfectly fine with me. On the other hand, if you're a boomer who missed out on the early days of pot smoking but still wonder if you indeed did miss out on something, retirement can be your perfect opportunity to explore this "high realm" of human experience.

If you have read this far into the book, I assume you do have a budding curiosity about how getting high with your loved one might expand your relationship and, indeed, your whole sense of what life is all about. It seems that everywhere I turn these days, seniors are talking in somewhat hushed voices about marijuana. Recent polls show that 59 percent of seniors support the legalization of pot, up from 49 percent just a few years ago. So there are already tens of millions of Americans over the age of sixty who for one reason or another have shifted their attitude in the direction of cannabis being good rather than bad in our society.

> Cannabis, like most potent things, can be used in a positive way and also in a negative way. The trick is to value the facts rather than the stereotypes and approach the whole idea of using cannabis in as wise and respectful a manner as you can muster.

In this light, I remember our neighbors around the block, Nat and Ruth. We'd become casual friends, but they knew of my work with cannabis and tended to maintain a clear distance from us. Then one springtime afternoon, as I was out walking, Nat called me over to his garden and offered me a beer. "How's things in the smoky zones?" he asked in his usual light mode.

I just smiled, not feeling at all attacked. "Oh, it's an old hippie's dream these days, what with all the new legislation popping up everywhere."

He sipped his Coors. "I hear they're going to start putting your stuff in my beer any day now," he said. "Just what we need – all the rednecks running around stoned on top of being drunk."

What could I do but grin and sip. "I'm with you! I don't know what the world's coming to, but it's coming at us real fast."

"You've been smokin' that whacky tobaccy all your life?"

"Started when I was twenty. I was never one to smoke when I got up, but yeah, three or four times a week, in the evenings mostly. Except when I had little kids, you know. And there were weeks or months that went by here and there without puffing. I suppose it's like you with your beer and wine and whiskey."

"Well, with your short hair these days, I'd hardly know you'd been a pothead all your life."

"It's served me well. I like being high, but I also like being dry. Balance is everything, wouldn't you say?"

"Well, I'm proud to say I'm past sixty now, and I've never smoked that stuff even once."

I grinned at him. "Congratulations."

"Ruth, too. She about chased her nephew out of town when she caught him puffing out here in the backyard."

"So I heard."

"Well, damn it, John. Now she's got it in her head that we should, you know, try the stuff."

"Oh?"

"Over my dead body, I told her."

"I hope not."

"She tells me that we can just order some, and it comes right to the door now."

"Yep."

"Crazy, making drugs that easy to get."

"You can order your beer to the door."

"Not the same."

"Right. Alcohol's addictive; it's one of the prime ruinations of people's lives. Weed isn't addictive like alcohol, and it makes you more peaceful rather than more violent – that's a bonus. And it expands consciousness rather than contracts it."

"Yeah, but Jesus used wine for communion, not pot."

"I was reading a report last week saying that the early Gnostics used magic mushrooms from the Lebanon woods in their ceremonies."

"What, now you want me taking psychedelics, too?"

I sipped. "I don't care what you do, Nat. But I've seen couples who'd ended up with nothing to say to each other anymore start smoking the herb, and then they start talking to each other again."

"So you're the one who put that idea into Ruth's crazy head?"

"No," I said. "But it's been in the news recently."

"So, what do you do? Just buy a pipe and stuff it in and go at it?" he asked. "Or I hear you can just buy pills and brownies and such and eat it."

"Well, if you're planning on trying it, probably best to smoke it first."

"Hey, I'm not talking about trying that stuff, Ruth is."

"I see."

More sipping. A Cooper's hawk suddenly flew right overhead; we could hear its wings flapping. "What's going to happen if we do?" he went on. "You're the expert. How about it?"

"I'm getting set to write a book on that so I won't have to keep saying it all over and over again," I responded lightly.

"Hey, I've got no interest in getting stoned and going crazy and chasing my tail. You tell me, what's the point in that?"

"Well, the point is that two people who love each other and know each other and care for each other can get into a rut in their relating and feel like the well's run dry," I told him bluntly, knowing Ruth a bit. "If you approach the muse of marijuana properly, you might open up and start having a new exciting phase of your marriage."

"What, wild sex times again?" he chided me.

"Quite likely."

"Not at my age."

"Definitely at your age."

"You mean the stuff's a – what's that word – aphrodisiac?"

"Lots of things can open up when you get high and shift out of your usual habits and mental patterns and so forth. You're pretty much guaranteed to have new experiences. And when you do this together, you can discover whole new realms."

"There you go again, talking like an old hippie."

I grinned back at him. "You bet."

We had that kind of conversation three or four times in the next few weeks. He seemed to hang outside waiting for me to take a break from writing and come out of my house and up the street. I felt inspired by his willingness, despite his prejudices, to keep asking questions and learning more about cannabis. When he and Ruth finally got around to trying the herb, they were well prepared – and except for an initial ten minutes when Nat had a spell of anxiety, things went well for them.

LETTING GO

In another situation, a just-retired CEO of a local company, whom I knew from around town, phoned me out of the blue one afternoon and asked for a formal appointment, thinking that I still worked as a therapist and saw clients in the usual manner. I explained that, like her, I'd retired from my earlier career, but I invited her over anyway to chat about whatever was on her mind.

She was reticent at first, hemming and hawing about what was bothering her. Finally she came out with it: "It's just hell," she confessed. "Reginald and I worked all our lives so we could retire and ease up, and now here we are – I've got all my art projects and my girlfriends I hang out with, and music and hiking and tennis, and Reggie is down at the golf course all the time. But I admit, we're already bored to death and getting on each other's nerves. And okay, yeah. Things could be better between us. We've got everything, and we're not all that happy."

I sat quietly and waited for her to go on.

"So, you know, you gave that talk about marijuana a while back that Reginald went to, and he thinks he wants to try the stuff."

"I see."

"No, you don't see! He's got all these books and keeps talking about consciousness expansion and spiritual awakening and how we're missing out on life. But listen to me – we go to church, and we have our religious beliefs. We know right from wrong, and I was brought up believing that God gave us our perfect minds and we're not supposed to violate God's creation with drugs!"

"If that's your belief, that's fine," I said evenly.

"Well, I surely wouldn't have allowed anybody working at my company to use drugs. What would the world come to if we let marijuana take over our whole civilization?"

"That's a very good question, and we still don't know the answer," I told her.

"But you're the expert. You tell me, what's going to happen if I try that stuff just to please Reggie?"

"It all depends."

"I'm not about to take something that makes me lose control."

"Then it's best to not use cannabis because it actually helps you do just that – to let go of trying to control everything."

"But if we let ourselves get out of control, we're likely to do terrible things."

"You're thinking of alcohol now, or amphetamines perhaps, and yes, they do tend to provoke out-of-control violence. But marijuana has been proven to make people more peaceful, if anything. That's a fact. Perhaps you can let go of controlling yourself and instead trust your better nature. If you're created in God's image and have faith in human nature, I think you can get high, relax, and enjoy life – and trust yourself not to do anything bad."

She sat there, thinking. "So you say I should take some of the stuff?"

"That's your decision. I would recommend that you get educated about cannabis and then decide. But I'll say this – marijuana has the gentle power to temporarily shift your experience in directions that most people find enjoyable, insightful, and rewarding. When you take it together with a loved one, it often opens up doors that will nurture your relationship on a lot of different levels."

"But it's still a drug."

"That's why it has the power to elicit a new experience."

"But what value is an experience if it's dependent on taking a drug?"

"Another good question. All I can say is that you grow through having the experience. That's its value. It's also just enjoyable and fun."

"Well, so is heroin, they tell me."

I sat back. "I'm not here to argue with you," I told her with a smile. "I don't care what you decide. But I'm happy to provide some guidelines if you want."

For her second visit with me, her husband joined us, and we talked through various aspects of their looming high experience. They made it seem like they were preparing to climb Mount Everest. And in fact, after I got them all set up, one night my phone rang, and it was her husband freaking out because she was freaking out.

He put her on the phone, and using basic therapist skills I quickly got her to turn her attention to her feet and wiggle her toes a bit. I also had her focus on her breathing and then on what she saw when she looked around her. Very soon she was calming down and delighting in something in her room – I can't remember what – that looked so beautiful to her. In ten minutes they were doing fine, and we hung up.

She came by several times thereafter, eager to tell me about their latest couples-cannabis episode. She announced that they'd had their first giggle fit since they were newlyweds, and she was now studying the physiology of laughter, so we talked all of that through. She said she had no idea that her husband had such a sense of humor – and also, somewhat hesitantly, she mentioned that they'd played around together like kids, you know, in bed . . . and also that they were into a whole new world of cooking together and were having feasts like kings every time they vaped.

Later on she told me they'd had a spiritual experience together that had changed them forever, she said. And somehow they were just being kinder with each other and more open to her daughter and grandson too.

MAKING THE DECISION

Everyone has their own life story, their own needs and hang-ups, their own pleasures, and so forth. Like I've said several times already, the great power and pleasure of cannabis is that everyone has their own unique experience with it, and each time it's different, as if the present moment is always new – which it is. We're living in a universe that's constantly changing. Our ego mind-sets try to establish permanence and predictability, but marijuana shows us the reality: each moment has never happened before and will never happen again.

Marijuana's effects can definitely scare away people who feel the need to stay in control all the time. The ego is afraid to let go and just see what happens naturally. But our deeper soul seems to yearn for freedom from that control. Sure, we often got punished for letting go when we were kids – that's part of the socialization process, which can be quite unfair and damaging to youthful spirits. Cannabis from this perspective is a liberating experience, where we set ourselves free to just be . . . and to flow with whatever inner experience comes naturally to us.

This "freeing up" dimension makes the cannabis experience especially interesting and rewarding from a therapist's perspective, which is why in the past I sometimes used it as a therapeutic tool. When approached wisely and mindfully, getting high can induce emotional healing by liberating a person from chronic tight control of the ego. And because we tend to be especially uptight when relating with other people, getting high with a loved one can set loads of healthy vibrant impulses free to express themselves.

I'd like to end this chapter with a list of questions that you can ruminate about if you're currently trying to decide whether you want to explore the marijuana muse for the first time or if you are already using it and want to evaluate whether it's a good idea to continue or to stop. There are phases of life when getting high is a great idea, and other times when it's not – and knowing when to pause is important.

> As you peruse these questions, you'll get maximum impact if
> you first take a few moments to pause and get centered inside
> . . . tune in to your breaths coming and going . . . and your
> whole-body presence resonating within the space
> of the room you're in.

Then, while staying aware of your whole-body presence, go ahead and read the first question, and just see what words come into your mind in response. There are no right or wrong answers. Just move through all the questions in order, taking plenty of time to let the questions awaken unexpected insights, and at the end, see what conclusions and realizations have naturally come to you.

1. Are you considering using cannabis for the first time?
2. Do you enjoy the effects of a couple of alcoholic drinks?
3. Is it easy for you to let go and be spontaneous?
4. Are you seeking some new fun times?
5. When was the last time you had a giggle fit?
6. Are you afraid to put your social mask aside?
7. Do you consider yourself a spiritual person?
8. How often is your mind quiet and at peace?
9. Do you like to pause to just enjoy the beauty of life?
10. Do you sometimes feel like you are on the edge of madness?
11. Do you yearn for deep insights into your life?
12. When was the last time you just goofed off for an hour?
13. Are you afraid to get high with marijuana?
14. Can you imagine feeling free to do whatever you want?
15. Are you wanting to make more heart contact?
16. Do you honestly trust your own self?
17. Do you want to be high with your loved one?
18. Would you like to be more engaged intimately?

19. Are you afraid to be emotionally exposed?
20. When was the last time you free-form danced?
21. Can you imagine having a great time while you are high?
22. Do you feel free to just say no to taking pot?
23. What does your heart say about using marijuana?
24. Are you ready to decide now?

> You can return to this list of questions over and over as your perspective on using marijuana evolves. Each question is designed to elicit an associative flow to new thoughts and feelings, insights and memories, imaginations and conclusions.

While contemplating these questions, you might want to "listen in" to see if you can at some point hear your own inner voice speaking to you, letting you know your deeper intuitive as well as logical thoughts and feelings about whether cannabis will be good in your relationship.

This self-reflective process can also be shared with your partner, if this works well for you. And if you do start using pot, return to this list of twenty-four questions often to see how your perspective is evolving.

QUESTIONS FOR REGULAR USERS

If you sometimes or often use cannabis with a loved one or friend, here are some further questions that will perhaps enlighten you regarding this use.

1. Is the way you're currently using cannabis good for you?
2. How many times a week do you partake?
3. What are the benefits you gain by using marijuana?
4. Are you still growing emotionally by getting high?
5. Do you often get high with your partner?

6. What happens when you get high together?
7. What would you like to have happen when you are high?
8. Do you think you use cannabis too often?
9. When was the last time you went a week without using cannabis?
10. How does using pot improve your life?
11. What do you share with your partner when you are high?
12. Has weed helped deepen your bond with your partner?

Run through these questions occasionally so that you can observe how your responses are evolving over time. Go through this list with your partner, too, if this seems like a good idea for you.

FOUR

Preparing to Take Off Together

After a period of struggle or hard work,
we need to rest and quietly look inward
to integrate and calm our emotions
and restore whole-body equanimity.
When calling on the muse of marijuana,
we have the opportunity to
change old thinking patterns by
observing and accepting ourselves
with an open heart.
We can transcend past traumas
by choosing to put aside the old
and embrace more hopeful feelings.

Whether you're a novice or a pro, if you've chosen to explore getting high with your loved one, whatever that relationship might involve, let's now advance. When you and your partner are ready to mindfully use cannabis to temporarily shift into a new shared experience, what basic procedure might be optimal for you? What preparations maximize a rewarding enjoyable cannabis adventure?

Depending on your city and state, you'll have legal options and hindrances to obtaining cannabis. Because the quality of your pot is important, I recommend finding a source whom you trust to advise you. In general, for our relationship-enhancement purposes, you'll want to use cannabis that is high in THC and low in CBD, but I strongly advise always having some CBD in the mix. A 2:1 THC-to-CBD ratio is often just right, but even a 4:1 ratio is fine. Just don't have too much CBD or you might drift off rather than stay alert and relate.

Once you have your cannabis in hand, there is also the question of how you want to ingest the herb into your system.

SMOKE IT: If you buy unprocessed dried bud to smoke (and get all the various cannabinoids found in this raw form), you can grind up and smoke the herb as a joint, just like in the old days, although rolling your own joint is sometimes challenging. You could also just buy a rolled joint at a dispensary for less than five dollars and puff away. This is perhaps the best first step for new users.

You can also get a regular smoking pipe at any smoke shop or online. Just stuff it and puff away. With a pipe, the key to success is remembering to inhale a mix of air with the smoke so that you don't get an overly strong hit, and also so you cool the smoke with some air before it goes into your lungs.[1]

Water pipes are cooler on the throat and lungs, and therefore perhaps the most popular way to smoke marijuana.[2] They are my own preference because I have a sensitive throat. You can find many different kinds online; note that the smaller ones work just as well as the large ones. Or you can buy a traditional Persian hookah if you want to get really sophisticated; smoking the herb in this traditional way gives you a lot of control over how much you take in (usually two or three puffs will do the trick – experiment!).

There's an added positive dimension to smoking marijuana with a partner. You're lighting the herb on fire and then inhaling the smoke from that fire. You're passing the joint or pipe back and forth, which in itself is an intimate act of sharing. And meanwhile, you're sharing space alone together, tuning in to each other's presence and current mood. I personally value all of this experience, but you'll want to feel out what your preference is, remembering that it can evolve over time. (And by the way, studies show that smoking weed once a day doesn't cause any health problems, even over the long term.)[3]

DAB IT: Hashish (the potent resin from the cannabis bud) has been smoked around the world for many centuries. Recently, refining techniques have been developed for generating sticky oil extracts similar to hashish. These oil extracts, or dabs, as they're known, can be fairly pure, coming in at up to 90 percent THC – that's very strong!

The sticky oil is extracted from cannabis buds with a chemical solvent, such as butane or carbon dioxide, and then processed to generate a variety of dab products, such as wax, shatter, budder, or butane hash oil. The usual ingestion method, called dabbing, is simple – you buy a dab sample, put a tiny piece on the tip of a pin or nail, heat this dab with a lighter until it is smoking, and then inhale the smoke directly or through a dab rig.[4]

Dabs have been popular in America since the 1960s, but the advent of more advanced extraction methods has led to a flood of cannabis concentrates that have accelerated the popularity of dabbing.[5] You get high almost immediately by dabbing, and the smoke from dabbing is fairly pure and easy on the lungs compared with smoking bud.[6]

VAPE IT: Vaping uses a handheld electronic device, much like an e-cigarette, to produce a vapor that you can inhale – and that, it is hoped, contains the chemicals you want to get into your lungs and bloodstream.

Dry herb vaporizers heat the cannabis to a temperature just below burning, generating a relatively cool vapor with effects similar to those achieved by smoking pot in a pipe or water pipe.[7] If you want to vape, a dry herb vaporizer is probably the best way to go, although it's usually a bit more expensive and requires more preparation than using a vape cartridge.

Cartridges are typically used with vaping devices known as pens. The cartridges are filled with highly concentrated extracts of raw cannabis bud.[8] You can also find vape cartridges that claim to contain pure hashish oil, but for ease of use and cost, most people tend to buy cheap refined THC/CBD cartridges.

The primary benefit of vaping with cartridges is that it is a very convenient method of consumption. Another plus is that you can vape in public and no one will know that you're using cannabis; you could just as easily be vaping tobacco in your vaping pen. The downside, in my experience, is that the concentrated extract in the cartridge has been through so much chemical refinement that it often carries pollutants. Also, the high that you get from vaping with a cartridge is somewhat different from the high you experience when you smoke or use a dry herb vaporizer. The many other naturally occurring chemicals that you'll inhale when you smoke, dab, or vape unprocessed marijuana are almost totally removed from the cartridges – and that does seem to make a difference.

If you are intrigued by the convenience of vaping, feel free to try this route. Many couples swear by their cartridge-based vape pens. And with a little research, you can understand the production methods and find products that are less processed than most.[9] However, for me and many others, the high that you achieve from these processed extracts seems to lack certain subtle psychological innuendos that would otherwise be present in the "pure smoke" versions of smoking a joint, smoking a pipe, or vaporizing the dry herb. You may want to take time to experiment with all of these methods to see how you respond to them.

For safety's sake, I should also mention that on the black market, where there's no government testing, many illicit manufacturers are producing and packaging vape cartridges that are, in fact, sometimes deadly. As reported by digital media company Inverse, Myron Ronay, CEO of BelCosta Labs, a cannabis testing lab in California, says that his company often sees "black-market products that contain unsafe levels of myclobutanil – a fungicide. When myclobutanil is heated, it releases toxic fumes, one of which is hydrogen cyanide. Small amounts of HCN are released when smoking cigarettes, but larger doses are lethal. HCN was a major component of Zyklon-B, the gas used in Nazi gas chambers. Unregulated products . . . have no one checking to see where that line is drawn."[10]

Black-market vape products, such as the notorious Dank Vapes cartridges, are never tested to see if they meet quality standards and are safe to use, so I strongly recommend avoiding them. If you adhere to these guidelines, you should do just fine with vaping.

DROP IT: You can also take cannabis drop by drop in the form of a tincture. A cannabis tincture is usually made simply by soaking ground marijuana bud in alcohol.[11] Tincturing is a time-honored process of making medicine that has been in use since ancient times on several continents, and before illegalization in 1939 in America, tincture of marijuana was a common patent medicine, sold throughout the country to alleviate arthritis, menstrual cramps, headaches, insomnia, and many other ailments.[12]

In contrast to highly processed extracts such as dabs and vape cartridges, a tincture retains most of the active trace constituents found in cannabis, just like whole-bud marijuana that you smoke. You'll feel the effects within five to fifteen minutes. And it's easy to take – it comes packaged in a bottle with a dropper top, which you use to place two or three drops under your tongue. You don't swallow the tincture; rather, you let it be absorbed under your tongue. In this way, the constituents pass directly into the sublingual artery, which takes them right up to your brain.

Another advantage of using a tincture is cost. At a dispensary, you can get a hundred-drop bottle for about twenty dollars. This means that you can get high for just thirty to fifty cents. And a tincture has a long shelf life; it will remain potent for up to a year.

For all these reasons, tinctures can be a good alternative for couples who do not want to smoke pot. But don't overdose; when you are first experimenting with tinctures, wait at least half an hour before taking more than three drops. Remember, more is not better – especially when you are taking cannabis with a partner, you want to get high, not knocked out.

> Overall, most people seem to report that tinctures don't deliver quite the same high as smoking weed and often seem weak in effect. This has been my experience. But perhaps a lesser high is just what you are looking for. Experimentation is key.

EAT IT: Many people think that drinking or eating cannabis is by far the easiest way to get high, and in many ways, this is true.[13] You simply buy cannabis-infused candy or another food product, gobble, and sit around for an hour or two until the effects manifest. But remember that rather than being high for an hour or two, you're going to be high for three to six hours – or more.

When you eat or drink a cannabis product, rather than smoking or vaping it, you begin an entirely different biochemical story.[14] Cannabis that you drink or eat goes down to your stomach and then heads to your liver, where it's broken down into 11-hydroxy-THC. As we noted earlier, there has been little research on the physical, cognitive, and emotional impact of this metabolite.

You can buy all sorts of edible cannabis with varying ratios of THC and CBD. Usually they are very potent, and it's very easy to overdose.

If you want to get high for a couple hours with your partner, eating or drinking cannabis extracts might not work well because of the one- to two-hour time lag before the onset of effects. Also, you probably won't get high at the same time as your partner because your metabolism won't run at the same pace. In contrast, with smoking and vaping, within a few minutes you're both feeling the effects together. This is an important consideration when you want to share an experience. Once again, though, it's your choice, so work out what's best for the two of you, and experiment with the options that appeal to you most.

Hold in mind that on the internet, most of the information you'll find on vaping and edibles is offered by sites that would like to sell you edibles and vaping equipment, so it's seriously biased. And that's a good reason, or set of reasons, that so many people continue to prefer unprocessed bud as smoke or tincture, rather than vaping or eating cannabis.

BEFORE THE SHOW

Once you've decided how you want to take cannabis, there emerges the follow-up question: Just prior to intake, what you might do to prepare mentally and emotionally for your shared high experience?

SAFE ENVIRONMENT: First, make sure you feel good together in the space you're going to occupy while you're high. There's no need to overly control your environment; just set aside time – at least an hour or two – when you'll be undisturbed and find a place where you'll be comfortable and at ease throughout. Have some good drinks at hand, and perhaps some music, poetry, or whatever appeals to you. But hold in mind that you will want to focus on your partner and whatever interactions arise, and not just zone out and watch a movie.

MIXING WITH ALCOHOL: You'll also want to discuss whether you're going to include alcohol in your high experience. The mix of the two generates a different high from using just marijuana.[15] You'll want to experiment to find out what you and your partner prefer. It's perfectly fine if one of you includes alcohol and the other abstains. Wine goes well with cannabis; beer might make you a bit drowsy. Hard alcohol seems questionable – certainly imbibing too much will muddy and lessen your "high together" time. And too much seems to be anything over two shots or glasses.

Side effects such as anxiety, hallucinations, paranoia, and so forth will be exacerbated by mixing alcohol with cannabis, so you may not want to include alcohol for the first few times you try the herb.

There's a saying going around that reflects a medical observation: "Weed before beer, you're in the clear. Beer before grass, you're on your ass." Why is this? Well, alcohol expands the blood vessels in the lungs, so you absorb more THC when you inhale cannabis smoke. Also, people who have been drinking tend to take deeper tokes when they smoke weed. In either case, blood levels of THC go up 10 to 30 percent if you drink first and toke after – so hold this in mind!

The effects of cannabis on blood alcohol are just the opposite. If you smoke first, subsequent alcohol levels in your bloodstream will be lower than they would have been if you hadn't smoked cannabis. This is probably because cannabis slows the movement of the contents of your stomach through the liver and into the intestines. Another fact: using cannabis regularly tends to reduce the adverse physiological and performance effects of alcohol through cross-tolerance. But that doesn't mean you can use pot to make you a better drunk driver.[16]

Alcohol often reduces inhibitions and helps people feel more spontaneous, which, combined with the similar effects of cannabis, can lead to relaxed fun times and often some great sexual interaction. But alcohol is a depressant, it's addictive, it impairs judgment far worse than cannabis does, and it actually reduces your awareness and ability to interact meaningfully.

Overall, combining one or two alcoholic drinks with moderate intake of cannabis generates a mixed impact that a lot of couples enjoy. Again, experiment to find out what you and your partner like best, and vary the mix whenever you want a bit of a change in your shared encounter.

UPRIGHT OR SUPINE?

Perhaps this is obvious, but it's worth noting: If you get high and stand or walk rather than sit or lie down, you'll have quite a different experience than if you are supine.

Studies have shown that being upright in general makes you more mentally proficient, more alert, more socially engaged, and so forth. Lying down activates the sleep reflex; being upright keeps you relatively awake. And of course, there are various gradations in between.

Sitting upright at your kitchen table, on your meditation pad, or in a chair outside will generate a different quality of consciousness from leaning halfway back in your easy chair in the living room. Lying down on your bed will shift you (and your partner) into more interior and often erotic realms.

So take a bit of time to consider where you want to sit, stand, walk, or lie down during the time when you'll be high together. This preparation can help greatly in guiding your experience. When you're high, you will often forget your options and just stay where you got high for the whole time. But shifting your location and posture can help shift you and your partner into a different mood and experience.

If you program your mind with several options before you get
high, then while you're high, you'll tend to remember
this posture variable and make a move now
and then together. Enjoy the shift!

In my opinion, the recliner chair is one of the greatest inventions for cannabis enjoyment. You can almost instantly go from sitting upright to halfway down to lying almost flat on your back. If you have two recliner chairs facing each other, you and your partner can begin upright, chatting with each other, and then shift halfway back for another, often more intuitive and dreamy experience where you can still see each other, and then, finally, you lie all the way back and drift into inner realms, communicating more by talking than by seeing. A sofa that holds both of you comfortably can also offer variations in posture, and of course, it offers the great opportunity of easy touching and so forth if you and your partner become thus inclined.

Lying on your back was described in ancient yogic sutras as a meditation posture of equal value to sitting upright; it's said to elicit deep inner journeys and lucid dreaming experiences that usually don't arise when you meditate in an upright posture.[17] I learned this from Osho, one of my early meditation teachers, who also valued cannabis in meditation (although with several cautionary suggestions that we will talk about later in this book).

THE PAUSE THAT REFRESHES

Once you and your partner are all set to take off on your shared journey, I have one final suggestion for your preparation: Get your preferred cannabis-intake system ready to roll and then, before ingesting, give yourselves a few minutes to let the dust settle and to tune in to your own inner presence. This process can be very simple, and it can include a meditative dimension, if you like. Here are some general ideas and guidelines; you'll also find several types of audio guidance programs on the High Together app as well (www.mindfullyhigh.com).

So . . . you're sitting together, and there's zero on your schedule for an hour or two, which means you can finally just kick back and do absolutely nothing except tune in to what's going on inside your own skin. Remember, if you're not aware of your own distinct inner presence, there'll be nobody home for your partner to relate with!

I recommend that you both agree to pause all relating activity for at least just a few breaths. Give each other breathing room to look directly inward and to reconnect with your own personal center of awareness. This is usually experienced not in the head, but in the chest and heart and belly – this is where you live, so to speak.

Many people find it difficult to stop being chronically fixated on sights, sounds, and thought flows and to simply focus within. That, of course, is what meditation is all about.

Perhaps both of you will want to temporarily close your eyes in order to initiate this preparatory phase. See how it feels to apply a bit of discipline to your mind as you sit still and temporarily aim your attention away from all the activity around you, and also away from all the constant chatter inside your thinking mind.

Take a bit of time to get centered and mindful in your body. Observe passively the ongoing flow of inner experience, even before any effects of the cannabis you're going to ingest touch your consciousness.

Traditionally, as we've been discussing, marijuana was taken into the body primarily through inhaling smoke into the lungs. The very act of taking the herb in as smoke naturally focuses your attention on the breathing experience. My recommendation is that even before ingesting, you focus on your breaths coming and going. Perhaps you both might count your breaths up to twelve and then back down to zero. This will give you several minutes of quiet inward experience.

> If you smoke or vape your cannabis, your attention will naturally focus on your inhalations (as you draw in the smoke or vapor) and your exhalations (as you blow the smoke or vape out).

Tuning in to your breathing before you partake will get you ready. You might also want to reflect on the biological fact that when you inhale marijuana, the chemical will naturally initiate its first effects down in your lungs, heart, and chest region – your heart chakra, in ancient yogic terms. So even before your brain gets its dose of THC, your torso will experience a shift. And heightened awareness of your chest, your torso, your heart, and your breathing will quite naturally prepare you for a deep experience.

Here's some beginning guidance to help you develop this breath-awareness habit.

〜〜〜〜〜

Right now, as you read these words, expand your awareness to become conscious of the actual sensation of the air that's flowing in and out of your nose . . . don't make any effort, just observe how your breaths come and go . . . all on their own.

Allow your awareness to expand to include whatever feelings you might find in your heart as you look inward . . . and notice how almost immediately you feel a shift begin to happen in your inner experience: suddenly you'll find that you're more "here" in your bodily awareness. Even while reading these words, you can also stay conscious of your nose and the sensation caused by the air flowing in and out with every breath you take.

As you continue reading these words and focusing on the sensations of breathing, observe clearly that even when you make no effort at all to breathe, you continue breathing in and out. When you reach the bottom of an exhalation, pausing for a brief second, notice that your diaphragm reflex will naturally keep you alive by gently provoking your next inhalation.

INNER VOICE OF GUIDANCE: When you tune in to your breaths as they come and go, you'll find that you naturally also tune in to your whole-body physical presence, from the inside out. If you want, you can now expand your experience to tune in to your inner voice of guidance and wisdom. Breath awareness is the foundation of meditation because you are choosing to just be quiet and passive and observe whatever's happening inside you.

When you pause like this before using cannabis with your partner, sometimes you'll realize that you're packing a raw bundle of chronic tensions, upset emotions, and scattered anxious thoughts. That's fine. A key element in getting high successfully is to stop judging how you feel. Instead, go ahead and give yourself permission to experience all your feelings – and also give yourself permission to let go of them more and more with each new breath.

As you continue breathing, you can give yourself permission to let go of whatever thoughts might still be floating through the back of your mind . . . and with every new breath, let your usual thoughts become mostly silent as your whole being opens to enjoy the emerging moment. Sometimes you'll receive new insights from your intuitive center. It doesn't matter what your particular religious or philosophical stance in life might be; just relax all of your ingrained tensions and habitual thought flows and experience your natural personal presence directly, through your senses and your inner awareness.

FOCUS PHRASES

If you and your partner would like a little more structure for this shared preintake phase, you can devote a couple of minutes to watching one of the twenty-four two-minute guided video experiences on the Mindfully High app and website. These videos are designed to help you shift your focus in an uplifting direction, both before you partake of the herb and also, if you want, anytime during your experience.

You'll find that the heart of each guided video is a focus phrase – a one-liner statement designed to aim your mind's attention directly toward a particular inner experience and realm of reflection.

Focus phrases are short powerful intentions that you hold in your mind by saying them silently to yourself. You'll find that when you're high, focus phrases can take on extra associative power and stimulate quite deep experience.

An effective focus phrase will aim your attention in key inner directions in just a few seconds. For instance, in the focus phrase we're going to consider first, the intent is to gently turn your attention toward good feelings in the present moment – right now. It uses the power of intent to transform your immediate experience in a direction you prefer. Here are the specific words that most powerfully initiate this shift to focusing on good feelings:

I choose to enjoy this moment.

If you not only read these words but also say them silently to yourself as you exhale, the words ("I choose to enjoy this moment") will shift your focus of attention exactly toward your intended target – feeling good in your body right now. When you're high while doing this, saying the focus-phrase words silently to yourself will instantly ground you into a more mindful whole-body awareness.

The second focus phrase in this series advances your awareness toward feeling good in the here and now:

I feel the air . . . flowing in . . . and flowing out.

Your experience of breathing is intimately linked with your emotions and inner "feeling" of who you are. Feel the air flowing . . . and you are instantly in tune with your emotions – right now. Do this together with your partner, and you'll each expand your personal bubble to include each other.

Once you've expanded your awareness to include the sensation of air passing in and out through your nose, there's a third focus phrase that will naturally expand your awareness another remarkable notch, so that you're suddenly focused not on a point in your body, but on your entire breathing experience. Just say to yourself:

I feel the movements in my chest and belly as I breathe.

As you say these words silently to yourself, they aim your attention down to experience all the muscles that are relaxing and contracting to suck the air deeply into your lungs and then blowing that air out again. Doing this consciously, you'll suddenly experience yourself as three-dimensional – as volume. Tune in to your throat . . . your heart . . . your lungs . . . your belly.

Saying these focus phrases silently, especially while high, will expand your experience exponentially because you're staying

highly aware as the effects of the THC interact with your deeper conscious experience.

A fourth focus phrase expands your inner awareness yet another primary "here and now" step:

I'm aware of my whole body, here in this present moment.

Once again you're directing your mind's attention in a very specific direction – in this case, toward experiencing yourself as an integrated and whole physical presence. The magic of focus phrases is that the very act of saying the words silently to yourself stimulates an instant expansion of awareness to include everything mentioned in the focus phrase – in this case, your entire physical being, right now!

A final focus phrase rounds off this mindful expansion of awareness in a beautiful way. I encourage you to say it to yourself often, as it's the sum total of the other four focus phrases – it's where meditation and cannabis will often take you, as all thoughts naturally become temporarily quiet and you enter that special mystic place where you're simply "being" in the present moment, not distracted by thoughts of the past or the future – the "high" place where new experiences can suddenly come flowing into consciousness:

My mind is quiet . . . I am fully here.

When you say these words silently to yourself, you elicit the experience you've just stated: your mind will respond and become calm, entirely in the eternal present moment. In my experience, marijuana does help us temporarily tap into this deep, satisfying, enlightening state of mind. That's why cannabis is called an insight drug.[18] Especially when you use focus phrases to guide your attention in this direction, you can actively create the inner space where deep experience can come to you.

There are twenty-four focus phrases in this program; enjoy each of them on the High Together app. Every time, you'll go deeper in the targeted direction. Here are five focus phrases we recommend both before ingesting cannabis and during the experience:

I choose to enjoy this moment.
I feel the air flowing in and out of my nose.
I feel the movements in my chest and belly as I breathe.
I'm aware of my whole body, here in this present moment.
My mind is quiet . . . I am fully here.

INTENT VERSUS SPONTANEITY

So . . . you and your partner have decided to get high together, and you've taken a few mindful minutes to settle in and get centered inside your separate awareness bubbles. Now what? You open your eyes after your inward focus, and there you are – together and ready. Well, maybe not quite ready.

You've almost certainly talked about doing this marijuana thing together. Perhaps it's your first time with pot, perhaps it's your first time getting high with this person, or perhaps you've gotten high a hundred times together but never quite with this shared intent. I'll be offering a dozen programs (in progress) you might want to do together before you get high to prepare yourselves in order to maximize the experience that's coming. However, be aware that the free spirit of marijuana can be hampered by too much preparation and by too much setting of intentions beforehand.

In most cases, once a couple has settled in and taken some time to turn their attention inward, the wise move will be to jump in, and not to overdo the preliminaries before the two of you light up and free your minds of habitual realms of relating. But after a short shared meditation there's one additional step that can be of great help: sit quietly together, continuing with your breath-awareness focus, and allow a few moments of relaxed open time to see if you have anything you want to share before you get high.

This step carries the intent of providing space for verbal sharing. But it's best to not push; there's no need to talk unless anything spontaneously pops into your mind and you want to share it before partaking.

We're going to be talking a lot about just this – talking. There are certain important communication protocols that, when applied to being high together, can make or break your relating experience. All of life on this planet depends on maintaining various levels of balance, and a conscious balance between talking and listening is one of the most important.

Too often, when high, one person tends to talk all the time while the other gets exhausted through too much listening. So throughout this program, we're going to regularly refocus on how you and your partner are doing in maintaining a balance of listening and talking.

Just before you partake of the herb and tap into the marijuana muse, I recommend that you and your partner focus on talking and listening for a few minutes. This will enable each of you to express whatever's on your mind and give both of you a chance to listen with an open heart, not interrupting the other person until they've spoken their piece.

This phase of sharing in a mutual conversation before getting high does two things – well, three. First, it enables you both to be cognizant of fairness and balance in talking and listening. This is very helpful practice for when you're both high and perhaps not so aware of the conversational pattern you're in.

You'll be amazed at how a relationship changes when this
element of fair and balanced listening and talking is
consciously developed, step by step,
into a social art form.

Second, you're allowing each other to speak whatever's on your mind so that you each get a feel for the other person's current mood and fixation. These factors will change each time. Sometimes neither of you will say much of anything during this phase; you can just sit calmly and enjoy the moment together. At other times one or both of you will need to express something that's on your mind, before you are ready to let it go and enter an altered state with each other. Just be sure to let your partner fully express what's on their mind without interrupting.

EXPANDING YOUR AWARENESS BUBBLE

The third thing that will happen when you chat a bit before cannabis intake is a further expansion of your personal bubble of awareness as you begin to more fully include your partner in your bubble, and vice versa. You do have an invisible bubble of awareness that you live within. Sometimes it's expansive, and you feel in harmony with the whole world. At other times you might feel depressed, anxious, or stressed, and your personal bubble collapses to almost nothing.

When you chat a bit before getting high together and also stay aware of your breaths coming and going, you have time to observe how you're feeling and to notice whether you're open to sharing space or collapsed and not open.

The very act of observation will generate a responsive shift toward relaxing, being more expansive, and allowing your personal bubble to include your partner.

Said another way, we're often so lost in thought that we're entirely out of touch with our hearts. The short breath awareness meditation with focus phrases will help awaken an expansion of the heart, leading you down into your heart feelings.

You can set the intention together of focusing on expanding and sharing your private awareness bubbles with each other. A conversation about doing this is always insightful. At the same time, as I mentioned earlier, let's not squelch spontaneity with too much structure. Always be open to unexpected changes in your well-laid plans when getting high with your partner. Sometimes you won't want to sit and chat – you'll feel eager to just light up, dab, drop, or eat your favorite cannabis concoction and get on with it. It's your choice – always!

FIVE

Tapping into the Magic

Following bouts of labor and self-control,
there comes time to relax and light up
and enjoy pure comfort and leisure –
which will initiate a feeling of
satisfaction and inner peace.

If you want to shift your perspective
or change your current mood,
feel free to employ the muse
to open your heart and mind
to greater understanding.

When the opportunity arises
to give birth to new experience,
take time to create a
warm secure environment
and then give you and your partner
unconditional love and support.

If you've used cannabis before, you'll probably find that the waiting period, after ingestion but before the effects manifest, is quite easy. You don't know what's going to happen, because that's the nature of the marijuana muse, but you have a general sense of what's coming, and you can relax while waiting for the first high moment to arrive.

If this is your first time, naturally you're going to feel a mixture of excitement and apprehension; that's perfectly normal. Your playful spirit is going to be eager to go on this adventure, while your ego is going to be concerned and perhaps a bit anxious about approaching the fatal moment of no return, when the muse takes over and you gracefully relinquish habitual control.

Perhaps the best move you can make while waiting for the cannabis transformation is to continue staying aware of your breaths flowing in and flowing out, while at the same time staying tuned in to the physical presence of your partner, so that you're fully "here and now" when the effects begin.

If you smoke or vape, the waiting time will be just a couple of minutes, perhaps up to four minutes. If you drop a tincture dose under your tongue, the wait can be five to ten minutes and sometimes fifteen. If you eat your dose, the wait can range from half an hour to over an hour. This makes partner coordination more difficult but not a total hindrance – you can hang out together for the interim or agree to come back together in half an hour or so.

A key principle to hold in mind just before the first rush of THC hits is that there are two base mind-sets – thinking or being – and you are always in one of them.

You're either engaged or at ease. You're either focused on a point or experiencing the whole at once. You're either lost in thought or enjoying your sensory surroundings.

I usually recommend that you shift into the "being" mind-set just before you begin to feel the effects of your herbal intake. In our society these days, we're mostly locked into constant action gear, very seldom pausing to catch our breath and quiet our buzzing mind, open our heart, and rejuvenate our energetic system. But to consciously flow into a cannabis high, it seems best to choose to make the shift into "being" mode as you negotiate what's sometimes called the "pot portal." This way, you're not going to be caught off guard, focused on a past-future thought, imagination, or memory, right when the marijuana muse taps you on the shoulder.

THAT FIRST WILD RUSH

As its active constituents (namely, THC and CBD) flow inward and upward and find neural receptors to lock into, the impact of cannabis on consciousness is usually quite sudden. If you're busy chatting with your partner, you won't be watching for this initial shift in your awareness. On the other hand, if you're maintaining your awareness on your breathing and your whole-body presence after you partake of the herb, you can consciously welcome the marijuana muse into your evolving experience.

You might want to play a game with this. See which one of you notices the effects of the herb touching you first. Just raise a finger when you feel that sudden shift. This joint attention to the process is always fun and brings you immediately together and focused in the same bodily direction. You'll also experience together how the muse tends to spontaneously snap your attention away from habitual thoughts and actions and toward the "doing nothing" state of experiencing the ever-new awakening into high consciousness.

I use the term "awakening" in this context because so often becoming high feels just like that; suddenly everything changes, the lights come on inside, and you wake up to a genuinely transformed state of consciousness that impacts the following four dimensions of awareness.

- *Sensory perceptions:* You might suddenly see, hear, feel, taste, and smell at a heightened level.
- *Emotion and mood:* You might become more aware of your breathing and your feelings as you experience more directly your present emotions.

- *Memories and imaginations:* You might spontaneously tune in to specific memories or imaginary visions that seem to come vibrantly to life.
- *Sudden explosions of ideas:* At the beginning of a grass encounter your thinking/talking function will often engage with bright new ideas and realizations.

Unless you purposefully choose to manage and direct the first few minutes as you get high, often your usual mental and social habits will continue to dominate and limit what happens. This is, of course, perfectly okay – but you can also talk about this tendency beforehand, and perhaps reach a shared decision to be quiet and at ease as the effects hit you, so that you're fully receptive to whatever new experience spontaneously appears. Sitting quietly together doing nothing when the muse first touches your consciousness can transform this beginning moment so that each time you get high together, something quite new is free to emerge.

> In this light, it seems that the best intent in the very first moments of a shared cannabis high is to choose to put a temporary stop to absolutely everything, including your thoughts, past memories, and future imaginations.

Instead, choose to focus on your breaths effortlessly coming and going, the physical sense of your body balanced in gravity's embrace, and the distinct flush of transformation as a bright awakening experience spontaneously happens.

BREATHING INTO THE RUSH

As the marijuana constituents gently enter and impact every cell in your body, you'll naturally flow into one of the seven dimensions of the cannabis experience that we talked about earlier.[1] Quite often you'll move through these different states in the order in which I presented them, but it doesn't matter at all if you pop out of this order. A client of mine named Jocelyne told me her story in this regard:

> Dave and I were expecting to maybe go through the talking phase and then shift into the fun of just enjoying sensory pleasures, but like a wave of bursting passion, we found ourselves in five minutes focused way down lower. It was like being teenagers again. Nothing was going to stop us from just totally indulging in the rush of surrendering to wanting each other – right away, not sometime down the road. Half an hour later we were lying on the rug and some pillows, totally spent and laughing at ourselves for being so crazy – and then, sure, we started talking and went into a deep place with each other, sharing some memories we'd kept buried about our earlier lives and lovers, and being open maybe for the first time about a lot of long-buried feelings. But that first wild rush of suddenly shifting into sex mode and throwing all plans and inhibitions to the wind – that was such an experience, and it all started because we agreed right in the beginning to stay quiet and tune in to our breathing, and that took our attention right into our genitals . . . and they were just too hot to ignore.

It's demonstrably true that when you get high, your breathing will usually lead you to where you most need and want to go. When you tune in to your breathing, you tune in to your whole body – and when you do this, you're directly in touch with your feelings.[2]

Physiologically, you can't really separate how you're breathing from how you're feeling because each emotion carries its own breathing pattern.

When you're feeling anxious and uptight, your breaths will be tight and shallow. When you're feeling passionate about something, your breathing will expand. When you relax, your breathing relaxes – but if you think for just thirty seconds about something that angers you, your breathing will shift into anger mode. Change your mental focus to imagine being on vacation on the beach, and your breathing will go right along with the imagination.

When you're together with a close friend or lover, you'll naturally observe how that person is breathing – and this in turn gives you a direct indicator of their inner feelings. Jocelyn described it this way: "Dave was just sitting in his easy chair after we toked up, and I was in mine, relaxing and enjoying my inner shift into that expansive feeling that grass always brings me. Then I heard Dave's breathing change slightly – and I immediately knew that sound and it just turned me on, just like that. He laughed, and I knew what was going on with him over there, and without thinking I let my own body do what it wanted to – I got up and went over to him, and yep, I was right!"

Regardless of how in particular you respond, the initial impact of the herb generates an alteration in your breathing experience and throughout your whole being. As those of you who already use pot know, at first your blood pressure will go up, your heartbeat will accelerate, and you'll find yourself feeling quite different throughout your body. Research shows that THC doesn't go just to your brain; it's taken in your blood to literally every cell in your body, and each cell will open its THC receptor portals and welcome the chemical into its interior realms.[3] Biologically, every cell in your body gets high, not just your brain!

This whole-body feeling of relaxation and pleasure is biochemically very similar to the flush of bliss that you experience when you have an orgasm. When you combine the two (as we'll see later) the inner experience is quite remarkable.

Observing the changes to your breathing as you get high is indeed powerful. It serves as a barometer for your body's inner condition, clarifying your current mood and energy.[4] If you stay focused on your own breathing and also pay attention to your partner's breathing and whole-body presence, you can enter effortlessly into a shared moment of expanded consciousness. You can connect not only through your words and actions but also at an immediate heartfelt level of intimacy.

~~~~~~~

For a few moments, let's continue to strengthen your power to stay aware of your whole-body presence, even right when the cannabis experience takes off.

While you continue reading the next pages, see if you can read the words and at the same time stay fully aware of your breathing. Feel the air flowing in, the air flowing out . . . and also feel the movements in your chest and belly as you breathe. You'll probably discover that you can understand the words you're reading and also stay tuned in to your inner presence. This is true expansion of consciousness.

As you read on, see if you can keep your awareness bubble in this expanded state of breath . . . words . . . whole-body presence . . . here and now!

~~~~~~~

HELLO, MUSE

Because it encourages us to turn inward, when we use marijuana as part of a couples experience, it can activate habitual psychological defense patterns such as avoidance and withdrawal. But if we allow it, the marijuana muse also encourages us to let down our guard and open ourselves up to vulnerability and honesty – and therefore to connection with our partner.

If you've mostly used marijuana alone, or if this is your first time trying the herb, cannabis might tend to shift you into a mostly inward journey. This is fine – unless you're with someone who wants to relate with you. As we'll see in coming chapters, sometimes even during a duo high it's quite appropriate to retreat into your own inner realms of individual experience.

But usually, if you've agreed to get high together, you'll want to maintain your intent to be outwardly focused, socially available, and intimately connected.

Our assumption in this book is that you do want to share your high experience. Especially if you begin your experience by expanding your bubble of awareness to include your partner, as we've discussed, you can use your partner's physical and emotional presence as the impetus to "stay here" rather than drift off.

By purposefully focusing on your partner as your inspirational muse, you can keep your attention directed outward quite effortlessly. But you do need to get clear inside your own mind and feelings that you are freely choosing to remain present and responsive – and this means that even before you get high and certainly right after, you will want to tune in to your own heart feelings and look honestly to see how receptive you are to your partner.

We talked earlier about how getting high with a partner is risky. It is! Marijuana can make you seriously transparent. It can also make you bluntly honest. You're liable to find out how you really feel toward your partner, beyond all social and intimate obligations. If you'd rather not look quite so clearly at your relationship, then yes, you may be more likely to just duck out of the encounter and direct your attention solely inward.

But I've found that the honesty initiated by marijuana does not break up relationships. It's quite the opposite, actually. By helping you temporarily let go of feeling defensive, cannabis can open your hearts and souls to a new level of closeness and mutual appreciation.

I remember a client telling me:

Last week, the second time we got high together, we had been arguing about something – I don't even remember what; I just remember feeling tight and contracted. But we had our plan of smoking weed together, and I went along with it. Len was feeling about the same. So we puffed and sat there not saying anything, still a bit angry at each other. A few minutes later we were just kind of staring at each other, impatient for the effects to start. And then . . . well, we just stared a long time hotly at each other – and then guess what? We both burst out laughing at the same time. And once we were done laughing, we talked and talked about how we'd been fighting just like our parents had fought, and how stupid it was to still be acting like them.

What's important is not to avoid whatever might arise between you as you get high. The thinking mind can always come up with a reason to argue with or be judgmental about your partner. When you are high, if you find your thoughts drifting toward negativity and pulling you down, you do have the freedom and power to let go of the upsetting fixation, quiet your mind, and relax into the high.

The trick is to remember to let your awareness of your breathing drop your attention down into your chest and your heart – and who knows, maybe even further down.

You'll find that the muse of marijuana is ready and eager to carry you along on its magic carpet into uplifting feelings, lighter ideas, enjoyable pastimes, and feelings of connection. And when you include your partner in your personal bubble of awareness, you will naturally flow into shared moments.

Your partner in smoke is, of course, probably having a somewhat parallel experience, and when you choose to look and listen and touch, you'll bring your separate experiences into congruency. Be sure not to think that you have to "do" anything at all in order to engage. That's the thing about getting high together; you're not agreeing to do anything at all except just that –to spend time together while high.

You're free to let go of all your usual busyness habits, and also to let go of feeling responsible for the outcome. You can put aside all ideas of what you should do or what you want to accomplish. Getting high is off time; it's free time to share space and love and attention with your partner. It's not at all goal oriented.

To just be with your lover or a friend, without feeling you need
to do anything at all – that's your only goal. Nothing is required
of you except maybe offering your loving attention. You're
finally free to just let go and be the natural you . . . and
then see what happens!

For most of us, letting go and just being ourselves runs opposite to all our social training, conditioning, and relationship habits.
But cannabis can be such a great therapeutic tool because when you
risk all and just be you, you can actually discover that you're a loving
person – you have the capacity to ease up and laugh about life, to
drop down and look to the heart of things, to open wide and let your
love flow!

You also have the capacity to drop your inhibitions and share your
most delicate feelings and intimate space with your loved one – and the
marijuana muse will be there to guide your flow of mutual exploration
into new realms.

*How are you doing with reading these pages and also still staying
aware of your breathing as you think and reflect and imagine?
Staying present in your breathing while you go about your life is
a learned ability – the more you practice it, the better you get at
it. At some point, breathing your way through each new moment
will become a habit – one that will transform your life!*

*You're probably noticing that you feel better when you stay
aware of your breathing. Even when you are packing constricted
emotions, when you stay aware of your breathing, those negative
feelings tend to ease up and let go. Blocking, avoiding, and deny-
ing painful or upset feelings only buries them and makes them
fester. But openly accepting them as you continue breathing into
them offers your emotional system a release valve – with every
new breath, your emotions will move toward achieving a new
balance. So as you read the next section, breathe on!*

TRUST

Trust. It's one of the primary human virtues. Trusting each other is the foundation of a relationship, and trusting yourself is a prerequisite to trusting others. Likewise with marijuana – you must consciously learn to trust the muse if you want to gain its support and guidance.

You may have learned not to trust alcohol because it let you down; it separated you from the natural values, virtues, and principles that you know sustain all human relationships on earth. But it's a big mistake to associate getting drunk with getting high. The muse of marijuana doesn't aim to get you intoxicated – unless you are compulsively wanting to get stoned to the point that you phase out.

If you aim to get high and have a great adventure, learning experience, and intimate encounter, that positive intent will naturally point your experiences in trustworthy directions.

If you let go of ego control, what will you do? What will happen? That's the question that leads you right to the question of whether you actually, deep down, trust yourself. When you first get high, it's a good idea to simply watch yourself and see what happens. That's how you develop trust: by putting yourself at risk, making yourself vulnerable and transparent, and seeing what you, in fact, spontaneously do.

In a similar vein, when you get high with a partner, you're going to find out if this person is trustworthy. I don't mean this judgmentally; don't sit there watching with critical eyes. Just see what feelings come to your heart when you open up and experience directly whether the two of you trust each other to be spontaneous.

I can't overemphasize the importance of learning to trust yourself, trust the muse, trust your partner – and even trust the world. Sure, people will let you down, bad things will happen in the world, and you'll mess up here and there. Trust isn't about being perfect. Trust is all about attitude and intent.

What you expect of life is usually what comes back at you –
and that certainly applies when you're high with a partner.

Either we trust human nature and look for the bright side in life, or we are distrustful and constantly fixate on the negative. To see that mind-set as a choice is in itself liberating, and your experiences that unfold with cannabis will be dependent on taking this leap to trust the muse of marijuana.

Consider for a moment how trust impacts your breathing. When you find yourself distrusting something or someone, your breathing becomes anxious and tense, perhaps even angry and aggressive. Because your breathing is tight, your oxygen intake is less than optimal, and you begin to feel not very good at all – and there you are, spiraling down into a bad situation.

It's the same when you get high. If you don't trust that the marijuana muse will help set you free to be more spontaneous and natural, then this lack of trust will make you feel anxious, uptight, defensive, and closed to new experience.

If you trust me to speak honestly to you about cannabis, and
especially if you trust your own instincts to guide you away
from danger and toward positive experience, then you can
relax and be open and receptive to good times . . . and
they will come to you.

In sum: When you get high with another person, be sure to tune in to your breathing to see if you're feeling trustful or not. Talk openly with your partner about this, if you want to. Accept your feelings, and also give them room to evolve. As you stay aware of your breathing, you'll find that you naturally begin to trust your own body. Be thankful that even when you're not aware of it, your breathing continues to keep you alive – that's something you can truly trust!

And this is where we effortlessly slip into more spiritual notions about getting high because it's just one simple leap of faith from trusting your own breathing to trusting the life force itself. You are being sustained! When you get high, you'll often have flashes of such realizations that seem quite obvious and even banal – but these core truths are, in fact, what underlie our foundational sense of trust.

> We can focus on the love-based goodness of human nature and use our attention to increase that goodness, or we can focus on fear-based bad elements of human nature and use our attention to boost that.

In general, studies show that marijuana tends to help people feel more loving and less hostile. It encourages inspiration rather than apprehension. The active constituents in cannabis naturally stimulate hormones that help us feel loving and trusting – and we can further accentuate this positive influence by choosing to embrace trust of our own selves, our friends, our community, and the whole universe. And . . . it's all an ongoing breathing experience!

SIX

Finessing the Chatterbox Phase

The muse often tickles the mind
and evokes flows of unexpected
insights, memories, plans, and vision.

Feeling carefree, secure, and loved
encourages us to extend gestures
and words of simple goodness.

Trust in your free spirit to speak
and you'll tap the courage and passion
to express what lies deep within.

And remember that listening
for an equal amount of time
is the essence of
true love.

From recent studies and cannabis folklore, plus my own observations while working with couples, it seems clear that most people tend to shift right into "head-buzzing" conversations when they get high together.

This free-flowing verbal buzz can be great fun. Inhibitions are lowered, and bright new ideas, insights, memories, and realizations may come tumbling out into the open.

Remember Danielle and Jim, the schoolteachers in chapter 1? After her first high experience with Jim, Danielle reported back to me that they'd soberly done the preintake meditation I'd taught them and then ceremoniously lit and smoked Jim's water pipe. Then they sat there, concertedly watching for the first signs of being high.

And then we suddenly popped almost at the exact same time into quite an extraordinary feeling. At first I seemed to lose touch with my breathing and body completely, even though you suggested that I make that central. Instead I got lost gazing for who knows how long at the magic dance of the candle flickering on the coffee table. Then without thinking I raised my gaze and looked up right into Jim's eyes for oh so long – and then suddenly both of us burst out laughing. He just looked so serious, you know, and I realized I was being so terribly serious myself – and at the same instant we both saw how funny we were, being so serious! We hadn't laughed like that for ages, not since the kids were born. And we went right from laughing to talking – about how we really needed to loosen up like this, and have some plain good fun again in our relationship.

She and Jim talked nonstop with each other for about twenty minutes, she recalled. The next morning, they discussed their "high insights" and found them surprisingly valuable.

Critics of cannabis scoff at high insights, claiming that they're never worth anything afterward, but this isn't true at all.

Cannabis is often called an "insight drug" because it breaks us out of habitual patterns and liberates the associative function of the brain so that it can entertain unique ideas and visions.

As mentioned earlier, when we take marijuana with a partner, one of the main first effects is the "chatterbox phase," where seemingly great ideas and realizations bubble up spontaneously, often as if under great exuberant pressure, and get vocalized. We never know when these flashes will emerge – all we can do is be open to them and let them flow out.

However, it's also well observed that the nonstop pot buzz of our great ideas can at times go on and on and become a bit bothersome, self-centered, and a detriment to deeper relating. If we become overly caught up in our own seemingly brilliant flow of ideas, memories, plans, and realizations, we can end up ignoring our partner's inner experience entirely. When we're fixated on expressing the rush of great thoughts flowing out of us, we often lose any sense of heart contact with our patiently listening friend.

Stream-of-consciousness chatter can be stimulating, insightful, brilliant, and fun but also sometimes in need of reining in.

We're going to talk often throughout this book about how to mindfully observe and perhaps modify such behavior, because learning to do so goes to the core of what constitutes a successful loving relationship, where we

1. stay aware of our sense of feeling connected;
2. regularly tune in to the other's presence and experience;
3. observe old conversational habits and inhibitions;
4. focus attention on our whole body; and
5. spend equal time talking and listening.

Before getting high, you'll perhaps want to talk about this "staying tuned in" theme with your partner as you share your deeper intentions and needs, and also act on fulfilling them together. Even in long-term relationships, all couples need to perpetuate the process of observing and transcending limiting communication habits if they want to grow into new realms of sharing.

CONSCIOUS EQUILIBRIUM

One of the main complaints that people who are *not* high have about talking with people who *are* high is that "stoners just jabber on nonstop and don't ever listen." This chatterbox "problem" is very important to address and transcend if you want your high encounters to be mutually enjoyable and fruitful. However, I don't mean in any way to put down the exhilarating chatter-buzz that so often hits right when you are getting high.

It's all a matter of balance, mindful interaction, and knowing when enough is enough.

And this brings up a clearly related theme – that of being not only a good talker but also a good listener. Relationships work best when there's mutual conscious awareness of sharing the stage: talking half the time, and listening half the time. Deciding together to pay attention to this back-and-forth "broadcast/receive" balance when you are high is one of the best intentions you can set as you develop in a successful cannabis-supported relationship.

One of the serious misconceptions of the marijuana high is that we lose all self-control for the duration of the experience. It's usually assumed that we simply can't control our chatterbox talking sprees. But as a long-term teacher of mindfulness meditation using cannabis, I can assure you that you do have the inherent power to assume control of your social behavior when you are high.

What's key is realizing that you have the choice to stay self-aware as you talk. Staying mindful that you have this choice is what makes all the difference!

If the chatterbox dimension is an issue for you, I recommend trying this: Turn your serious talkaholic dilemma into a fun game to play when you are high. First, before lighting up or otherwise taking your cannabis, openly talk about this chatterbox theme. Discuss which of you tends to talk the most, and how you both feel about that. The discussion can in itself be a challenge because most people are defensive about even considering that they're sometimes a conversation hog. But if you ignore this theme, chances are high that you'll suffer from a bothersome imbalance in your conversations when you are high.

Let's look at why one person often talks overmuch while the other person listens overmuch. Chronic passive listeners tend to come from families where they weren't adequately listened to; instead they were dominated by a brother, sister, or parent and grew up resenting the fact that their voice was not valued. This "nobody listens to me" attitude and assumption can become ingrained and mostly unconscious, but it needs to be openly dealt with for the health of your relationship – and when you are high, it reveals itself, and thus opens up an opportunity for addressing it.

Solution: Beforehand, consciously agree that you'll signal physically when you've listened enough and are feeling fatigued by taking in so much information and chatter from your partner. Then, when you are high together and the time comes that you've listened enough, just raise your hand with palm outward toward your partner, signaling that it's time to end the one-way flow of words.

> The talker can, of course, feel free to finish the thought and then should gracefully become silent. The listener then can have an opening to speak.

This agreement to purposefully honor the "I've had enough for now" hand signal will prove a great additive to your conversations – and that's true whether you're high or not. What you're seeking to attain is an active state of verbal equilibrium, where there's a healthy balance between listening and speaking.

It does take energy and attention to listen to someone talking about their inner experiences. You're having to imagine and attempt to comprehend all the images and ideas the other person is expressing, and this is definitely mental work. For a while it's fun and interesting and even enlightening to listen to your partner remembering or brainstorming while flying high. But at a certain point, especially when you're stoned, you'll feel your attention waning and your breathing getting tight – you feel trapped, but you don't want to be rude by interrupting and demanding either silence or your own time to speak.

Here again, the ability to maintain breath awareness while high saves the day. If you're feeling as if you can hardly breathe, this means that you've taken in too much talk for too long at one time. You need a break.

So just gently and with a smile raise your hand, palm outward, with a slight nod to express your honest need for silence, for breathing room, for an end to the chatterbox buzz. If you've communicated about using this raised hand routine beforehand and experimented with it a few times, you'll both find it perfect for gracefully shifting. You'll consciously establish a fair and healthy balance between talking and listening in your relationship.

The fine art of listening while high is something you'll want to practice until you fully master it, and here are the guidelines that I've found most valuable to establish as a habit when listening. First, don't think that you have to come up with a response when your partner is telling you something. Very often, they're not wanting advice or an argument or any other response; they're just expressing something that needs to come out.

Talk therapy is just that – the therapist remains quiet throughout and lets the speaker fully express an inner memory, feeling, or condition. The healing process isn't generated by clever analysis of the therapist or friend; it's generated internally and often quite spontaneously within the speaker. You as the listener have only one role: to quietly hold your attention on the speaker while they talk.

But it can be harder than it might seem to remain quiet and not interrupt or offer advice or analysis. To facilitate this art of listening, I suggest the following: while your friend is buzzing with inner thoughts and monologue conversation, your primary job is to stay aware of both your own breathing and your whole-body presence – at the same time!

This technique is called the "two-at-once silencer" because as soon as you split your attention between two quite separate sensations – the feeling of your breathing and the feeling of your body, such as your feet on the floor – all thoughts inside your head automatically stop. It's the same trick I teach in my book *Quiet Your Mind* and the associated app program, and I call it mental judo because it is a method of using a natural effortless function of the mind to achieve an otherwise arduous goal.[1]

Try this for yourself right now. As you read these words, expand your awareness to include the sensations of the air flowing in and out of your nose . . . and at the same time, also be aware of your left foot . . . and for good measure, also be aware of your right hand . . . and as you come to the end of this sentence, see if you can continue to stay aware of your breathing, your foot, and your hand and, at the same time, think about anything at all. If you can, you're way ahead of me. And if you can't, that's how you can stay quiet in your mind while your buzzing friend is talking up a storm.

You'll find that if you practice this mental judo to quiet your mind while listening, you'll end up not feeling drained. In fact, this little inner meditation on your physical presence will serve to recharge your energy.

THE "BOING!" MOMENT

In a related theme, many people get upset when they get high, start talking, and then lose the thread of their conversation. We call this the "marijuana gap," and it's a universal phenomenon. Cannabis will set you off enthusiastically talking about something – anything at all – but then you might pause a moment to catch your breath . . . and not be able to pick up the thread of the conversation. Your mind just goes blank. You might say, "Umm, what was I talking about just then?" Your partner might not remember either.

This sudden loss of short-term memory, as we mentioned earlier, is part of the trade-off you must deal with when you get high. You simply lose your train of thought; you come to the end of your flow and get caught in the marijuana gap. When this happens – when you seem to just drop off the edge of your conversational cliff – it's usually wise not to fight it. It's better to shrug it off rather than struggle to pick up the drift of the conversation.

You can agree beforehand with your partner that if you hit a marijuana gap, you're free to indicate that you're letting go of that conversational thread. Set up a code word that you say when this happens. We say "Boing!" to gracefully bounce out of the verbal flow, and then both of us can take a conversational breather and let it all gracefully go. As we do this, of course, another topic can pop into mind, and off we go again. Or following a "Boing!" we might take the quantum leap beyond talking and shift into perception mode, now focusing on our sensory experience.

This works equally well when an idea pops into your high mind that leads you into inner thoughts and memories that begin to bum you out. If you're expressing this line of thought, and you realize you don't really want to continue focusing in that negative direction, set up the code word "Boing!" and just let that thought or conversation go. We're trained never to abruptly drop out of a conversation, but when we're high, it's very helpful to be free to let go of an unpleasant or negative buzz. Just agree that when this happens, you can simply say "Boing!" and end that thought riff.

This situation arises often when we're high because the associative flow of the mind is being stimulated with a rush of memories, imaginations, ideas, and so forth. Sometimes we get led into ugly memories or disturbing imaginations, and we need to be free to drop off that thought wave at any time. If you talk about this beforehand with your partner, there's no reason to feel embarrassed because you suddenly don't want to talk further about a particular theme, or because you suddenly can't remember what it was you were talking about a moment ago. Just say "Boing!" and you can both effortlessly move on. Perhaps you might enter into a bit of silence. Tune in to your breathing . . . and give the other person open space to begin talking about a new thought flow.

> You'll find that the "Boing" moment is contagious. Your friends
> will start doing it too, high or not, and in all conversations you'll
> gain the freedom to break off from what you're saying when
> you feel you want to, no questions asked.

Marijuana does alter how we converse, and one of the downsides of talking while high is that you might forget what you were just talking about. But hold in mind that losing the thread of the conversation is only important if you're trying to "act normal" and sound logically coherent. When you're high, yes, there's always going to be a trade-off. You're temporarily sacrificing some short-term memory and logical coherence in order to gain the freedom to abruptly follow new exciting associative threads. When you get high together, you're quite obviously agreeing to let go of your habitual ways of thinking and talking in the hope of accessing a more mysterious, free-roaming, intuitive function of the mind. That's the giant plus of being high together.

> When you and your partner are sharing this early chatterbox
> phase of a shared high, you're both experimenting. You're
> inviting the marijuana muse to affect your brain in ways that
> may make you seem temporarily a bit incoherent or dumb –
> but at the same time, you're entering into a portal of
> consciousness that can lead to you to explore some
> of the more intuitive realms of sharing.

Each time you get high with the same person, you have the opportunity to evolve into new ways of conversing together. You may want to talk about your shared experience after your marijuana high is over so that you can come to new understandings of what works best when the two of you are high together. Just always hold in mind that you are relating through mutual respect and compassion and seeking new ways of sharing your inner realms with your partner.

CANNABIS GIGGLES

As we saw with Danielle and Jim, along with the chatterbox buzz of words, during that first wild rush of the marijuana muse, very often something quite different and remarkably important can spring into being: the marijuana giggles![2] This is an involuntary wonderful whole-body release of tension giving rise to an instant sense of euphoric well-being and contentment that can last physiologically for up to an hour.

When you are high with a partner, even when you are right in the middle of a serious discussion, one of you can suddenly get emotionally tickled and start laughing outright. Usually this ignites shared giggling in the other person.

I recommend that when you are high, you let go of the social rule that it's rude to giggle. Instead, be ready to simply surrender to this primal, spontaneous process of the human body. And remember, you're not laughing at your partner, you're laughing with them.

By "marijuana giggles," we don't mean just an occasional chuckle. We're talking about getting carried away by an uncontrollable giggle fit that might leave you both delightfully rolling on the floor like little kids, convulsively overwhelmed by a mutual laughing fit.

Why does cannabis stimulate giggling? Marijuana boosts the levels of serotonin in your brain, which, in turn, elevates your mood. Shifting into a mildly euphoric state can spontaneously activate a giggling response even if there isn't a particular reason for the giggle. It's been shown that THC's cannabinoids stimulate heightened activity in the right hemisphere of the brain, causing increased poetic and metaphoric activity, and this can lead to seemingly outlandish and paradoxical thought patterns, which, in turn, provoke a response of hilarity and giggles.

As a therapist, I've come to hold shared giggle fits in very high regard. They provide much-needed emotional release of buried tensions and are a built-in mechanism for breaking beyond inhibitions and overly serious attitudes.

Medical research shows that giggling temporarily lowers your blood pressure, reduces stress hormone levels, gives your abs and other muscles a great workout, improves cardiac health, boosts your T cells and immune system, triggers the release of endorphins to lower pain, and leaves you with a general sense that everything in your life at that moment is just fine.[3] In other words, when you feel a giggle fit coming on, welcome it as your very best way to improve your health and mood.

THE GIGGLEGASM

Giggling is similar in many ways to sexual release, as we'll explore in a later chapter. Giggling is an accepted social expression of the basic orgasm response. It's sometimes called a *gigglegasm* in the same spirit in which a rush of meditative realization is called a *buddhagasm*. As in full orgasm, with a gigglegasm, all seven energy centers of the body (the chakras) fire off at once, resulting in a deep, satisfying discharge of accumulated tension. The sensation is usually a pure delight as you surrender control and let the muse tickle your innards.

Unless your childhood was terribly restricted, you probably indulged in many mutual giggle fits with your friends. But

you may have been punished for such raucous loud
outbursts, especially when you were in school.

The marijuana muse provides the blessing of bringing this primary healing discharge back into your life – and it's one of the most rewarding experiences to share with a partner! Just remember that when you're giggling, you're not laughing *at* your partner in any way; you're just surrendering to a much-needed outbreak of hilarity.

There are now therapy methods that openly provoke laughter as a means of emotional release. I studied under Chuck Kelley (the founder of Radix Therapy) in my own therapy training and learned, from the tradition of the great Wilhelm Reich, how to elicit a prolonged flow of laughter in my clients.[4] This training ran parallel with what I'd already learned from getting high with my friends and indulging in a great many giggle fits. It definitely gets the job done, blowing ingrained inhibition fuses and releasing a lifetime of buried tension.

CAPTURING YOUR BRILLIANCE

Each new time you get high with your partner, you'll flow into a unique expression of the liberating chatterbox phase as your inhibitions and contractions get put temporarily aside and you surrender to the insights that the muse of cannabis can spark. Trusting this muse, welcoming the buzz, and at the same time staying mindful of your experience – this is the challenge.

And what about all those great ideas that you'll share with your partner during a high chat? Yes, you'll forget most of them afterward because you're not busy establishing long-term memory traces. You'll be fully engrossed in hearing how you express new ideas that come springing out of a seemingly infinite womb of insights. So many people get upset about losing the brilliant ideas they had when they were high – but that's quite easily remedied.

First, with a little practice you can learn to pause after expressing a great idea, consciously tell yourself you want to remember that idea, and then think it through again so that it becomes embedded in long-term memory. Practice this "high memory" process a few times and you'll get good at it. A bit of discipline, even when you are high, can be of great value. If you make the effort, you can usually remember a great idea the day after your high time.

Also, I advise keeping your cell phone handy when you're high. If you have a great idea that you want to remember, go ahead and express it out loud, using your phone to record it – got it! Later, you can review your ideas and separate the wheat from the chaff, as my granddad used to say – you can determine what's worth saving versus what's a throwaway.

My observation is that it's usually best to capture the first few great ideas that come to you, recording them on your phone, and then to just go ahead with the experience and let the rest of your thought flows come and go on their own. Return your focus to your partner and your inner feelings, and don't fixate on catching all of the many great ideas.

ALLOWING FOR THE NEGATIVE

It may seem a bit strange to welcome anything negative as part of the chatterbox dimension of getting high together, but it has its rightful place in your experience. Over the years I've found the following suggestions of great value for couples getting high together.

Especially if you haven't had a chance to catch up with your partner over the course of the day, you might want to include in the chatterbox phase (if you naturally have one) a bit of free conversational time to share with each other the high points of your day. It's an excellent opportunity to reflect on what you've done and to discover the day your partner has had – all through the marijuana window, which invites associative thinking and insights. When you share consciously in this way, with the listener giving full attention, you'll find that hidden meaning and deeper significance tend to arise. Of course, you must both remember to honor each other by allowing each other to speak without interruption and listening attentively.

Most people do their best to stay positive with this type of exchange so that they do not pull the high experience down, but I recommend the opposite. Take a few moments to blow off any negative pressure inside you. Give yourself, and equally your partner, the freedom to express what's been bothering you on any front. In other words, share the golden opportunity to complain!

When you give each other permission to share the negative, you clear the air between you, discharge buried feelings, and reveal all of you. Just be sure to allot limited time for complaining – and raise your hand when you've heard enough. Fall silent afterward, and just relax into whatever pops up next. Almost always it will be positive.

PAUSE AND REFLECT

While you were reading this section, were you able to stay aware of the air flowing in and out of your nose? Let's expand this one more step to prepare for when you're high with your partner:

While staying aware of your breathing experience . . . the air flowing in . . . the air flowing out . . . expand your awareness to include your whole-body presence . . . and tune in to the feelings in your heart.

Now begin to imagine that you're with your partner, and you're getting high together. As you imagine the effects of the cannabis hitting you, imagine that you continue to stay aware of your breathing and feelings as the marijuana magic occurs. . . .

And now imagine that instead of immediately starting to buzz with thoughts and conversation, you continue to stay calm, aware of your breathing and whole-body presence . . . and also aware of your partner doing the same. . . .

And now imagine entering into the buzz of a great conversation – with you talking some of the time, then your partner talking, using the hand gesture to shift back and forth . . . and perhaps imagine having some fun and giggling together as well. . . .

~~~~~~~~

SEVEN

Coming Fully to Your Senses

Each of us is an opening for
God's creation to flow into us
through our senses.

It's said that we are
the eyes and ears of God
as we use all our various senses
to absorb as much beauty
as we possibly can!

In the world of shadow and light
we may often encounter the unknown
as we discover through our senses
that we and nature are one whole –
and by sharing our sensory delights
with the universe,
we can feel fully at home in this universe.

We often think of getting high as a mostly passive physical experience, where you just stop moving and trip off in an interior flow of experience. Maybe you and your partner get caught up in an initial buzz of chatting, eagerly recalling something that happened earlier that day, sharing flashes of insight, reliving upsurging memories. But at some point, one or both of you might get tired of the head-tripping and remember that you're free to silence the mental chatter whenever you want to.

You can then spontaneously shift into focusing your attention on the pure pleasure of present-moment perceptions – the overt sensory realm of consciousness.

Marijuana is prized for its ability to shift your mind's focus into sensory appreciation mode.[1] Suddenly it can seem that the world around you has come alive and you're seeing with fresh eyes – everything becomes more colorful, more beautiful, artistically touched. Words fall away, the mind becomes silent, and you become pleasurably engulfed in whatever natural or man-made beauty surrounds you on all sides.

What's going on here? Scientifically, as a report from the National Institutes of Health states, "THC stimulates neurons in the reward system of the brain to release the signaling chemical dopamine at levels higher than typically observed in response to natural stimuli. This flood of dopamine contributes to the pleasurable 'high' that those who use recreational marijuana seek."

In other words, when arriving in the brain, cannabis carries the biochemical power to amplify the pleasure of pure perception. You experience the world around you with fresh, innocent eyes – and are often stunned by the beauty surrounding you.

You might, for instance, realize that you've been chattering nonstop for ten minutes . . . so you consciously pause and quiet the mental buzz, and then you shift your focus outward and tune in to an enchanting perceptual experience. In a couple getting high together, this shift may happen to one person first, and then quite often the partner, having noticed the other person's sudden shift into quiet perception mode, will do the same. Suddenly both of you are tuned in to the "gazing" function of the brain, seeing and hearing and breathing and smelling, happily absorbing the shared sensory universe that surrounds you both.

This nonverbal act of sharing the abundance of beauty all around you is a primary bonding process in and of itself. And it often expands into more fully taking in the other person's physical presence through mutual eye-gazing and heart-connecting. Or perhaps the two of you might get up and stroll around together, enjoying flashes of aesthetic beauty.

This shift into movement can lead to more intimate movements as well, goofing and touching and hugging and kissing and so forth. As the Rolling Stones pointed out in their famous cover of a traditional gospel song, "You gotta move!" As long as you stay immobile or caught up in verbal exchanges, your relating experience will remain mostly mental, not physical – you're stuck in your head. But as soon as the chatting stops and you allow your attention to shift into perception mode, opportunity emerges in a variety of whole-body sensate realms.

> Marijuana delivers a number of "inner pops" as your focal attention shifts. This transition from a mental focus to the magic of whole-body sensory awareness can feel gigantic – suddenly there's space, volume, touch, sight, sound, and physical pleasure!

As thoughts drop away, as past and future temporarily disappear and the present moment becomes everything, you are set free to discover your expanding capacity to be fully here, mindfully present, and even spiritually attuned . . . perceptually merged with all of Creation. It's one thing to engage socially and intellectually with your partner, exploring new philosophies and realizations, imaginations and memories. It's quite a noticeable pop when this cognitive fixation drops away and you both become alert and aware as organic bodies embedded in a host of sensory delights all around you.

For a few moments after reading this paragraph, see what happens when you look up from the page, tune in to your breaths com-

ing and going, and then, even without a cannabis high, simply let your eyes feast on whatever you see around you that's beautiful . . . and notice that you can be aware of both inner and outer experiences (breathing and seeing, for instance) at the same time. . . .

TASTE

It's well known that cannabis increases appetite; when we are high, we do tend to get the munchies. Why is this so? The body naturally produces ghrelin, a hormone that stimulates appetite, in the stomach, pancreas, and brain.[2] THC also stimulates the production of ghrelin, which makes you feel hungry. Ghrelin also boosts the pleasure we experience from food, heightening our enjoyment of cooking and eating even a simple repast. Before getting high, you might want to set out something to cook, so that if the hunger reflex should suddenly come over you, you can move into the kitchen and delight in cooking and eating.

TOUCH

The sense of touch is the first sense to develop in the womb and plays a primary role in helping an infant bond with its mother.[3] To "feel good inside your own skin" is considered the height of well-being. Right now, as you read this paragraph, if you expand your awareness to include your whole body, what you're doing is shifting your awareness to the sense of touch at the skin level and also deeper into your sense of position and volume in space.

The whole notion of "be here now" involves being tuned in to your sense of touch – your remarkable inside-out experience of being present in your own skin.

As we've discussed, when you get high, you can focus in myriad directions – and your choice of a focal point determines your experience.

If you shift into sensory mode, you tune in to a vast realm of direct interaction with the outside world. Each finger pad, for instance, is loaded with remarkably sensitive nerve endings. And much of your body is covered with tiny hairs that transmit touch sensations to the brain to process as experience.

Touch is associated with a vast storehouse of personal memory – memories of being touched before – and there are loads of emotions linked to every type of touch. Cannabis helps you tune in to this level of experience. It also increases your sensitivity and pleasure related to touch, and this can be a major element in your cannabis experience, both when you are alone and, of course, when you are touching your partner.

Touching is vital to intimacy, so taking the time while you are high to tune in to your skin – your largest organ – can be highly rewarding, to say the least.

Cannabis is often praised for its ability to relieve numerous kinds of pain. THC has the ability to muffle the neurotransmitters responsible for causing pain. It also alters the transfer of anandamide, an endogenous compound that contributes to the body's regulation of pain, as well as hunger, mood, and memory.[4] CBD can be helpful for pain relief because it reduces inflammation. Through these and other mechanisms, and primarily by influencing how the brain responds to pain stimuli, cannabis dampens our experience of pain.

Many people who suffer from chronic pain find that when they are high, they feel less pain, regardless of why. In addition to the proven effects of THC and CBD on your biochemistry, perhaps it has something to do with cannabis's ability to boost your mood and sensory pleasure. When you feel good inside and outside, pain – or at least the worst of it – seems to drop away. You become free to have fun touching and otherwise interacting with your loved one.

To activate the sense of touch, all you have to do is focus there! Run your fingers along a surface, touch your own face, reach over and stroke your partner's hand . . . what you focus on is what you get!

HEARING

It's universally agreed that marijuana makes music sound clearer, louder, and better, and it certainly augments the pleasure we feel when listening. That enhanced pleasure seems to come not from a change in our physiological hearing system, but from how the brain processes the sound.[5]

Just to begin, pot alters how we experience time, and music is all about time intervals. Music is based on harmonics and overtones; it's a resonance that permeates the body, not only through the ear but also through the skin – we feel music all over! Adding weed to the listening experience, with its associated boost to our mood and our enjoyment of sensory stimulation, definitely amplifies the pleasure.

After we listen to a tune a few times, most of us tend to get a bit bored with the repetition. But with marijuana, our memory often fades quickly, and each time we hear the piece as if for the first time. This is a primary positive effect of temporarily shorting out our memory function. In fact, it is a remarkable trade-off for that memory reduction . . . the experience is always new!

Instead of listening in order to compare with a known musical memory, we can relax fully into enjoying the present-moment sensory event.

Cannabis alters the functioning of the occipital lobe, where we interpret sensory events, and this enables us to have a fresh encounter with our favorite music again and again. And THC, as a recent study indicates, increases the pleasure we feel from listening to music – or, indeed, to birds singing, wind blowing, or a friend talking.[6] Listening to music together can be a wonderful pastime for a couple, but make sure it doesn't dominate your relating. Take a breather after a few songs, and take time together to just "be," without any external stimulus. That's how to encourage the marijuana muse to deliver something new.

If you're a musician, even a casual at-home strummer, you might find that playing a tune for your partner can become a powerful experience and awaken unexpected associations. As a recent study concluded, "Cannabis produces psychotomimetic symptoms, which can connect seemingly unrelated concepts, an aspect of divergent thinking considered primary to creative thinking."

This "thinking outside the box" effect is one of the primary reasons that cannabis is used by so many creatives in their work. Even if you're singing a simple folk song that you've sung a hundred times before, when you're on grass, that song can come alive – and the act of singing and playing the tune can give both you and your partner great pleasure and inspiration.

GAZING

Our visual apparatus dominates our sensory inputs. We receive around 75 percent of our sensory data from our eyes. Although people report that while using cannabis they see more intensely, with more pleasure and discernment, it doesn't appear that marijuana affects the physical visual system – except that as blood pressure drops, the iris expands, giving the eyes a different appearance.[7] Sexual arousal does much the same.

Health-wise, cannabis offers neuroprotective, antioxidant, and anti-inflammatory effects, which can be helpful in improving cell survival in the eyes and encouraging eye health. It may help slow degenerative eye disorders such as retinitis pigmentosa and macular degeneration. Just getting high regularly seems to provide these visual benefits.

Vision-wise, you have two basic and opposite ways in which you use your eyes to see the world. First, you can focus both eyes together on a point and zoom in on it, seeing just this one particular thing, and shifting your focus to another point as needed. This is how we usually use our eyes, and when you're high, you might want to notice when you're looking at the world in this detail mode.

But you can also see in an entirely different way: you can let go of "point fixation" and instead relax and take in the scene before you as a whole. Seeing "everything at once," it seems, is the gaze of lovers, of people looking at a sunset, of meditators . . . and very often of people who are enjoying a cannabis rush as they look at the world around them.

I encourage you to experiment with this way of seeing because it's a portal to a vast realm of visual experience that simply has no chance of happening when you're focused on a point. You'll find that you often slip naturally into seeing "everything at once" when you're high. But you can learn to make the shift consciously, as an act of visual volition. Here's some guidance:

After reading this paragraph, put the book aside for a few moments and look around the room you're in. Notice how your eyes shift from one item to another, and how they focus not on empty space, but on a surface. Observe how you choose what to look at. Notice how your attention tends to leap quickly from one interesting item to another, rather than looking at one item for any longer than is needed to process the visual information. And now . . . begin to develop your ability to see everything at once by gazing in front of you, without the intent to focus on any particular object out there. Instead, focus a few feet in front of you – in open space! At the same time, tune in to your breathing so that you're focused both outward, into the open space in the room, and inward, into your breaths coming and going. Continue holding this dual awareness for a few breaths. . . .

If you do this when you're high, you'll immediately pop into an altered way of experiencing both the space around you and your own interior space. Space on this planet means air. You're focusing on the volume of atmosphere in the room you're in, rather than the things on the surface of that room. When you focus on things, you're in "doing" mode, busy gathering useful information to process and help you survive. Once you process that visual information – job done, move on.

> When you let go of working with your eyes, you also
> have the freedom to ease up, stop working, and
> use your visual experience to just
> enjoy the world around you.

A happy balance would seem optimum, but most of us have been pushed and programmed and otherwise coerced in our social conditioning to stay fixated on things, on surfaces, rather than enjoying the whole at once and experiencing the volume of the room.

If you pay attention to this shift from point fixation to seeing the whole at once, you'll find that when you're high, it tends to happen a lot – and when it does, usually you move into a bliss state. Why? Because you've let go of your ego's chronic workaholic control of seeing, and instead you're looking just for pure pleasure. A great deal of your brain takes a break, enabling you to shift into nonwork pleasure mode for at least a few moments.

When seeing "everything at once" you'll probably at some point find yourself looking into your lover's eyes with this gaze. Couples gazing has become quite a phenomenon recently, but I remember, even way back in my life, going to encounter group meetings and being instructed to simply look for five minutes into a stranger's eyes – and having remarkable experiences. I encourage you to talk about doing this gazing with your partner, and to explore what happens. Be sure to take time to talk about the experience afterward.

You might find that you begin to hallucinate different faces on your loved one's face. This is perfectly fine and often insightful. Don't take the faces that appear seriously. Your subconscious mind will have a heyday projecting archetypal faces; just relax and enjoy the show. And you can look at anything around you in this same "everything at once" mode as you allow the outer sensory data to intermix with your memory and imagination to create a unique experience.

SCENT

This fifth sense seems to be dwindling rapidly in humans; it is the least active of our senses. Over 70 percent of the human population lives in smog, which dulls any sense of smell. And our survival is no longer strongly dependent on being able to smell what's around us. The olfactory sensory neurons in the nose tend to stop working if we don't focus on them, and with age this sense diminishes much more rapidly than the other senses.[8]

The loss of smell is called *anosmia,* and often it is not reversible.[9] Sometimes something as simple as a viral infection or a bad cold can cause the olfactory receptors in the nose to conk out – and not return to normal.

In the days of our ancient ancestors, this would have been a major problem; like most animals, we once depended greatly on our sense of smell. Even as recently as a couple of hundred years ago, most people still lived in rural areas, worked outdoors, and tuned in regularly to all sorts of changing scents that would indicate weather alterations, seasonal shifts, and so forth. Now we're indoors most of the time and forced to breathe stale air from air-conditioning and forced-air heaters that leaves the air, if anything, smelling dead and bad, so we just tune out our sense of smell.[10]

Marijuana can reverse that trend. People often report that when they're high, they suddenly become able to smell more acutely and enjoyably – and it's a great rush! There's nothing like smelling spring-time breezes, fresh piney forests, or salty seaside air.

Our hearts naturally leap up when we behold a rainbow in the sky, but the same effect holds true when we smell new-mown grass or bread just out of the oven. When good fresh smells become vivid and alive, we naturally celebrate.

Notice that smelling and breathing are inseparable; as you breathe in, the air flowing through your nose activates the olfactory sensory neurons. So once again, tuning in to your breathing while you're high is a good way to optimize your experience.

The olfactory nerve runs from the top of your nasal passages a short distance to your brain and the olfactory bulb in the limbic system. From there, the olfactory information stimulates memories and primitive animal instincts that can provoke action – and at the same time a rush of pleasure.

Right now, or when you're high with your partner, play this fun scent game to awaken shared scents: Imagine that you're in a meadow full of springtime flowers . . . now imagine that you're in a gym during a basketball game . . . and imagine that you're at the beach smelling the gentle sea breeze . . . imagine that you're sitting down to eat your favorite meal . . . imagine the scent of your lover. . . .

YOUR SIXTH SENSE

Your sixth sense is your ability to sense your own body position and whole-body presence – where you are in space, where your various body parts are as you move, and other interior aspects of body awareness. Biologically, this sense is called vestibular awareness or proprioception.[11] It's what enables you to feel grounded and balanced in gravity and to maintain your upright posture on the planet.

We hardly notice this sixth sense, but it's crucial to our balance, movement, and whole-body sense of presence.

When I suggest that you tune in to your whole-body presence, this sixth sense is what I'm aiming your inner attention toward. Maintaining this whole-body awareness while moving through space and time can become a major activity while you're high, and especially when you're in physical motion. You probably already know how good it feels to be lighthearted and dancing freely to music, especially with your partner. Just taking a walk while high can be blissful, generating a remarkable sense of well-being and pleasure in the body. And of course, lovemaking is all about whole-body awareness.

Your sense of touch is mediated by your skin, which is rich with nerve endings that constantly communicate with the brain about what is touching you – its texture, temperature, pressure, and so on. When you get high, you can tune in more deeply to this subtle yet basic whole-body awareness. Many people report that they're mostly out of touch with this level of physical awareness. Getting high can reawaken this primal sense of your own presence. Just tune in to how your skin is a giant membrane, like the membrane of a living cell, holding you within its comforting embrace . . . for all of your life!

~~~~~~

Right now, as you read these words, feel free to expand your awareness to include your sixth sense of whole-body presence . . . breathe into this sensory experience . . . tune in to being balanced exactly in the earth's gravitational field . . . notice how you now feel more here, more engaged in the world around you.

Now let yourself imagine your partner, wherever they might be, also engaged in experiencing their sense of balance and whole-body presence by tuning in to this sixth sense. Imagine that, like you, your partner is feeling fully present in their bodily here and now . . . aware of where they are and how they're moving in balance with gravity . . .

You're both always sharing this same feeling – in fact, all human beings and all other living creatures are. It's one of our primary experiential links with each other. So see if you can stay aware at this core level, even when you're relating or thinking.

~~~~~~

SENSING THIS MOMENT

Overall, one of the main positive impacts of cannabis on human experience is this heightening of all our senses. In a very true way, you become more human, more natural, more grounded in our earthly realms of being when you get high and tune in to all your senses. It's great to chatter on and on with ideas and imaginations when you're high, but it's also truly blissful to allow the marijuana muse to retarget your power of attention away from brainy activity toward sensory awakening.

Suddenly shifting from a cognitive buzz into sensory experiencing can feel very much like a spiritual awakening.

Most of what makes us feel good is related to our senses, be it eating a great meal or running along the beach or dancing away the night or making love. We all know how unrewarding and even downright depressive it can be, for instance, to have sex but stay mostly in our thoughts rather than dropping down into pure bodily sensory pleasure and engagement.

So let's remember to regularly take advantage of the fact that cannabis tends to tune us in to our senses. Let's remember to "come to our senses" as often as possible! Put bluntly, how else do we usually engage with our partner, if not through our senses? Even when brainstorming an abstract idea, we communicate through sight and sound. It's true that we tend these days to get lost in thoughts and tech and head-tripping. Marijuana can very beautifully help us come to our senses.

As you continue reading, expand your awareness first to your breathing and whole-body presence . . . and now also tune in to whatever olfactory inputs you might smell at this moment . . . and notice that breath awareness always involves this shift into sensory awareness. . . .

As you continue reading, expand your sensory bubble to include whatever sounds might be coming into your organism through your ears . . . and experience your sense of time flowing by, in relation to what you are hearing. . . .

And, of course, also notice how your sense of eyesight is continually bringing new sensations into your brain. . . .

Tune in to your awareness of your body as an integral vibrant whole, sitting and breathing and maintaining its posture and balance while you're doing everything else. . . .

And . . . here you are!

EIGHT

Tapping Eros Transformation

Embracing the miracle of life
while embracing our lover
brings us directly into union
with the pure infinite pleasure
of being one with our Creator.

The muse of marijuana
is surely a devotee of the vast
realms of delight and discovery
that open to us every time
we open our arms and hearts
to provoke erotic adventure.

Sex and spirit are made
for each other!

As we just saw, tuning in to the world around you while you are high helps you tap into the pure pleasure of being alive in a body that's busy receiving multiple sensory inputs. As these sights, sounds, ephemeral scents, and tactile feelings stimulate aesthetic appreciation and artistic joy, they can also quite naturally encourage your awareness to drop down deeper into the feelings in your heart, and then on down into that most wonderful cannabis effect of all: sexual arousal.

Experiencing a sudden rush of sexual energy is, of course, not just a marijuana occurrence. A beautiful flush of eros is often stimulated by music and dance. It's great fun to crank up the stereo and tune in to the muse of movement and rhythm, of harmony and disinhibition. And whole-body dance movements made in synch and proximity with your partner are definitely enhanced by marijuana, as unexpected energy comes surging into conscious enjoyment.

Through physical and emotional expression, this charge can be readily shared on the dance floor, especially if you're in a living room, bedroom, or backyard where no one's watching and the sexual muse is free to express itself fully. Other variations on movement, such as yoga and stretching, are also wonderful ways to shift into whole-body enjoyment. And of course, dancing, stretching, or doing yoga together can become just the first erogenous step into deep sexual union of whatever type you prefer.

Full sexual expression can unfold in a seemingly infinite number of spontaneous variations. The question here is: While you are high, what is the best way to mindfully approach and release such a wild, volatile phenomenon as sexual passion?

Specifically, when your erotic charge has been stimulated by getting high together, how can you flow with your sexual energies to maximize mutual satisfaction? In addition, what's the optimum strain and dose for such sexually charged relating? And how can you integrate your sexual relating when you are high into other key components of a lasting relationship?

Research scientists are just beginning to have the legal freedom to conduct experiments exploring how cannabis impacts the sexual response. Dr. Monica Grover of Asira Medical, a specialist in family medicine and gynecology in Manhattan, reports conservatively,

"Consumption of small quantities (of marijuana) prior to sex may increase libido in female patients, which in turn can release positive endorphins and increase vaginal lubrication."[1]

At Stanford University, researchers Dr. Michael L. Eisenberg and Dr. Andrew J. Sun recently conducted a study on the effects of cannabis on sexual activity: "68 percent of the women in the sample reported more pleasurable sex with cannabis, 16 percent said it ruined their sexual experience, while the remaining 16 percent were undecided or unaware." In terms of men, "65 percent said cannabis enhanced their sexual experience, 23 percent said it didn't matter one way or the other, 12 percent had no significant feedback."[2]

In another survey, "72 percent of a female sample said marijuana always increased their erotic pleasure, while 24 percent said it sometimes did. Almost 62 percent said it enhanced the quality of their orgasms and their libidos in general. Additionally, 16 percent disclosed they purposefully puff pot prior to sex."[3]

For both men and women, the drug most commonly used in association with sex still seems to be alcohol. In a British survey, roughly 60 percent of both genders said that they often consumed alcohol before sex. Cannabis was the second popular choice, with a third of men and about a quarter of women saying they sometimes used it before sex. Third was MDMA, or ecstasy, with around 15 percent of men and women having taken it at least once before sex.[4]

Different strains of cannabis will have various effects on your sexual experience. For instance, many people say that very-high-THC strains (rated at 20 to 30 percent THC), such as Sour Diesel, Harlequin, Dream Queen, Blue Cheese, Goo, Kali Dog, Shining Silver Haze, and Skunk XL, are best. However, there's a great deal of constantly changing hype about which strains and hybrids are optimal, so don't get too caught up in thinking there's a "best strain" – in fact, it's often best not to get overly blown away by strong weed when you hope to make love. Sure, keep the THC over 15 percent and the CBD considerably lower, but hold in mind that you have your sexual charge already in place, and the cannabis is just an additive to your natural erotic flow. The same holds true for combining pot and booze; remember what we discussed earlier about how alcohol impacts a high mood. Unless you purposefully have the urge to just blow all your fuses in a wild party night, do keep the alcohol down to a couple of drinks, in most cases, and the marijuana to a few puffs or the equivalent amount of tincture or edible dosage.

My observation has been that eating cannabis, rather than smoking or dabbing it, usually reduces sex drive, but there are the notable exceptions of couples who want a lazy, hazy long evening. . . .

BEYOND SEXUAL ROUTINES

You are, of course, a unique sexual being, but you also belong to a species with fairly definite sexual behavior programmed into your genes – and cannabis seems to have a preordained biological potential to impact your sexual activity. In this chapter, I want to delve into how you and your lover can tune in to THC-boosted sexual flows in the body. We're also going to explore how to awaken all seven of the energy centers (chakras) in your body at once, so that they can fire off in unison during the pleasure of sexual relating.

Marijuana has been used for thousands of years in the kundalini yoga tradition of Hinduism and Buddhism to stimulate a higher sexual charge in the genitals, in unison with full-chakra meditation and mutual awakening.[5] (For more details on kundalini yoga, see my book *Kundalini Awakening.*) A dozen or so years ago, my yoga master friend Dee Dussault originated the term "ganja yoga" (*ganja* being Sanskrit for "cannabis").[6] And currently a growing number of yoga teachers are including cannabis as part of the yoga experience.[7]

But even without any formal training, you and your partner can explore how cannabis naturally leads you into unexpected expansions of your erotic life.

You probably already know from your own inner experience that when you make love, it's not just your genital region (the second chakra) that drives your experience. Certainly we hope that your heart (the fourth chakra) also comes alive and resonates energetically with your lower regions as you become aroused. And your fifth chakra region – in the throat, vocal cords, mouth, tongue, and lips – is also important in manifesting the sounds you make. The other chakras, too, each have their part to play in sexual arousal and activity.

But all too often, while we are making love we stay fixated in our minds, memories, thoughts, and imaginations. We run on automatic pilot with our lover, mostly acting out old erotic patterns. This is one of the main reasons that couples tend to share less sexual intimacy as time goes by – they're simply tired of routine.

Couples can readily learn to use marijuana as a magnificent disrupter of such ingrained and limiting romantic behavior.

Sure, particular strains of cannabis might have a stronger effect on libido than others, but the primary activating element when you combine pot and sex is going to be your shared intentions, your willingness to open to new experience, and your readiness to risk the possible embarrassment of being caught psychologically and emotionally naked – but then, isn't that what making love is all about?

If you like, we can take a moment here to consider your own habits and potential when you are high and making love. We saw earlier how human beings are always either busy doing something or doing nothing at all but easing up and just "being." When you move toward sexual relating with a partner, do you ever first pause together and just "be" there with each other, without any action?

We saw in previous chapters the importance of quieting the mind, stopping habitual activities, and shifting into the "seeing everything at once" sensory mode. This is such an important shift when you are making love because it allows your whole system to drop out of past-future thinking, remembering, and imagining.

When you temporarily stop everything and "be" quietly still
together, you drop deeply into your own body's presence. With
this "embodiment" shift, you tap into the full power of your
sexual response.[8]

Everything we've been learning and exploring thus far in this book
has led us to this point of applying a wise approach to mixing cannabis and lovemaking. We're going to look more fully into interesting
research on this theme, but first, to keep our discussion quite personal,
here's a beginning exercise you can do right now, if you like (you'll also
find this guided session on the High Together app):

〜〜〜〜〜

*After reading this section, pause for a few moments, perhaps close
your eyes, tune in to the air flowing in and out of your nose
. . . and begin to imagine that you're sitting close to or are in
bed with your partner. Now imagine or remember how you usually go into action to express your sexual desire. What are your
habitual "moves" when you're being intimate?*

*Now imagine that you both stop doing anything at all.
Instead, experience just sitting or lying beside your loved one
. . . breathe, and tune in to your inner sensations . . . set yourself
free to do nothing at all. Just experience your own physical and
emotional presence, and the presence of your partner breathing
quietly with you. . . .*

*Now, see if you naturally, without any thoughts, "shoulds,"
or preprogrammed sexual intentions, begin to respond internally
to the presence of your loved one. Your body and your partner's
body are energetic powerhouses; they resonate and radiate with
emotional energy even when you're doing nothing at all. Tune in
to this natural resonance of attraction between the two of you. . . .*

*And now . . . begin to imagine what might happen when
you let your body move effortlessly into subtle action . . . let your
whole being shift into its natural flow of sexual expression, all*

on its own. Notice whether you like this spontaneous approach to
the beginning of a sexual interlude as you delve into the infinite
mystery of erotic attraction and union. . . .

REEFER MADNESS REVISITED

Traditionally, the combination of "sex and drugs" has had a bad reputation in mainstream America, even though the same combination often carried very positive associations for many young people. Slowly we're gaining factual evidence that will help adjust attitudes appropriately, but many people still harbor entirely outdated prejudices against mixing weed and orgasm.

In 1936 the U.S. government released a propaganda movie, called *Reefer Madness,* that was designed to frighten everyone away from ever even once trying marijuana, which the movie portrayed as a narcotic that drove you crazy and made you a sex fiend. For decades this movie was the main reference point for parents trying to make sure that their kids never tried the "killer weed."[9]

When I was studying the impact of LSD on the brain in the late 1960s, parallel research was also being funded by the NIH to see whether pot reduces testosterone levels and libido levels – that is, whether it's bad for sex. That's what the government wanted to find, and sure enough, an initial research paper claimed that marijuana reduces blood levels of testosterone dramatically, by up to 50 percent.

This was an upsetting statistic for pot smokers at the time because testosterone fuels the sex drive in both men and women. The study was loudly reported in the news media and cited hundreds of times as a proven fact by law enforcement and education, as well as religious and government officials. It's still cited today to scare kids away from smoking grass. After all, who wants to lose their sex drive?

But then more studies were performed in several countries, and a flurry of reports on marijuana and testosterone were published in the late 1970s demonstrating zero significant suppression of testosterone by marijuana and also no significant loss of libido or sexual impairment even when the herb was used frequently. A number of highly respected studies in the 1990s expanded on these findings, showing that the biochemical and psychological effects of pot on lovemaking are both diverse and often unpredictable.[10]

Specifically, what they found was that for some people, some of the time, cannabis can be strongly sex inhibiting, whereas for others it's definitely sex enhancing – with far more people reporting enhancement than impairment.

One study showed that over two-thirds of subjects reported increased sexual pleasure and satisfaction, along with an enhancement of emotional closeness and enjoyment of the more tender aspects of sexual intimacy. However, over a quarter of the subjects reported a reduction in sexual focus and activity while they were high. These people tended to be introverts, personality-wise; they withdrew from social relating while stoned, and often they withdrew from their own bodily awareness as they turned inward to imaginary fantasy adventures inside their minds.

In a 2003 study, Canadian researchers interviewed 104 adult cannabis users about their sexual reactions to marijuana. Did it increase libido? One-quarter said it "often" or "always" did; 40 percent said "sometimes"; and one-third said "seldom" or "never." About half called the drug sex enhancing, but almost half said it was not. One-third said sexual enhancement was a key reason they used weed, while over a third said sex played little, if any, role in their use of the drug.[11]

In another study, about half of the interviewed subjects claimed that marijuana boosted their libidos, increased their sensitivity to touch, and enhanced their erotic pleasure, while a quarter said it reduced these factors. And in a recent *Psychology Today* survey, 68 percent of the responders reported that marijuana enhances their sex life, whereas 12 percent reported that pot shut down their sex drive. It was generally agreed that dosage and the strain of marijuana definitely influenced the sexual experience, with most agreeing that as dosage went up, sexual activity dropped.

So what's going on here? Obviously, cannabis doesn't always induce the same sexual response in everybody all the time. Your mood, energy level, expectation, emotional involvement with your partner, and other factors strongly influence the sexual outcome.

Meanwhile, research in Australia has now clarified quite solidly that even long-term use of pot doesn't erode a person's biochemical sexual drive or ability. Sex hormone levels aren't different in marijuana smokers versus nonsmokers.[12]

I haven't yet found any research examining whether eating cannabis has a different effect on sexual expression than smoking it. From related studies, we can predict that results will vary greatly based on the person and the situation. I personally find my libido dropping considerably when I eat cannabis (which I seldom do). In contrast, smoking it, especially when I haven't made love in a couple of days, predictably nudges the experience toward a sexual expression, with the THC serving as a strong positive sexual additive.

Especially when a person eats pot or takes a high-CBD mixture, the higher the dosage, the lower the sexual charge will predictably become.

By the way, you'll find loads of new cannabis products purporting to boost your love life. One of them, a candy bar called High Love, mixes cannabis with several other supposed aphrodisiacs – and, of course, chocolate.[13] Feel free to experiment with such products, holding in mind that your expectations and current overall energetic condition will determine much of your experience.

CANNABIS FOCUS CHOICES

In the midst of all the unanswered questions related to cannabis and sex, we can still identify a set of choices that help determine whether you will feel sexually excited when you get high. At the heart of these options is the most obvious choice: whether you focus your attention inward and away from any social or intimate physical involvement, or whether you choose to stay tuned in to your partner's physical presence as you shift into the marijuana mind-set. You can easily go either way – into social withdrawal or into sexual intimacy. And that choice is always present, especially if you remain mindful of your options as you get high.

These options of where, how, and whether to engage sexually are often determined by how you feel inside your own skin – by the level of energetic charge you're packing, and especially where in your body you're holding your focus of attention.

Clearly, if you focus entirely on a buzz of thoughts and imaginings that are happening at the top of your spine (the fifth and sixth chakras), you're probably not going to notice or stimulate anything happening down at the bottom of your spine in the second chakra, the sex center down in the genitals.

We've already seen that when getting high, most people tend to allow their ingrained focal habits to manage their attention. If there's an obvious genital charge or an eager sexual partner, attention will drop downward naturally, but often people stay caught up in that initial head buzz, with habitual thought flows dominating and lower-down sexual regions receiving no stimulating attention at all.

Of course, there's nothing wrong with head-tripping when you're high, nor with letting your attention randomly shift here and there with no conscious intent or direction. Jumping spontaneously from one mental focus to another is one of the true gifts of the marijuana muse. However, most people in an appropriate situation with their sexual partner do often want to focus on the immediate physical pleasures of sexual relating.

One of the best ways of consciously choosing to focus on erotic rather than intellectual realms is to move through a quick mental refocusing process that leads you down through your body from head to genitals. Here's the process, in case you want to do this as part of a high experience (it's also available as an audio guide on the High Together app):

~~~~~~~~~

Sit or lie comfortably, side by side if you're doing this with your lover. Let your eyes close, if you want to . . . and notice where in your body your attention and energy seem to be focused. . . .

Now consciously shift your attention to the air flowing in and out of your nose or mouth . . . and allow this focus on your breath to expand to where you're also aware of your head . . . and your throat . . . and your lungs as they expand and contract with each inhalation and exhalation. . . .

Now expand your awareness to include your chest . . . and your heart . . . notice the emotions you feel arising as you experience your whole torso. Relax your tongue and jaw, and let your breathing deepen . . . and see what feelings you have in your heart right now. . . .

Now expand your awareness another notch to include both the feelings of warmth and love in your heart and also the feelings of power and desire in your belly . . . take a few breaths to really settle down into your body and focus on whatever rising energies you might discover. . . .

Now go ahead and expand your awareness downward to include the sexual realms awaiting in your genitals . . . let your pelvis rotate a bit as you inhale and exhale . . . feel whatever charge of sexual desire and passion you might tap into with each new breath. . . .

Now, to activate all seven chakras at once, bring your attention to the top of your head, and allow your whole-body awareness to drop down step-by-step from the top of your head . . . to your throat and mouth . . . and on down into your heart . . . and into your belly . . . and down into your genitals . . . and all the way to the bottoms of your feet. . . .

Let yourself feel how the sexual energy in your genitals naturally merges with the power and desires in your belly . . . and feel how this raw sexual hunger rises up spontaneously into your heart and merges with the more subtle but essential feelings of yearning and compassion there. . . .

When you're ready, you can end this whole-body focusing process . . . and continue to enjoy and express the great feeling of balanced whole-body charge and presence. . . .

WHOLE-BODY DOPAMINE

When you focus on thinking, a lot of blood immediately flows up into your brain to fuel this mental buzz. We saw earlier how cannabis often stimulates excited talking about great ideas, memories, imaginations, and plans. In this chapter, we're seeing that you can shift your focus elsewhere in your body and, in so doing, generate quite a considerable change in how you feel and relate.

Regardless of where you focus in your body, cannabis provokes the secretion of dopamine, serotonin, oxytocin, and endorphins (the happiness hormones), which, in turn, impact the brain. This same biochemical effect is also happening throughout your whole body because your bloodstream carries the dopamine everywhere inside you. This hormonal shift actively enhances your overall sensory experience and propensity to get excited sexually.

In fact, a complex symphony of chemicals orchestrates that radical flush of sexual arousal associated with a cannabis high. The human sexual response is definitely a whole-body event.

ENTERING ETERNAL TIME

There's yet another element that influences high sex: the curious way in which your sense of time becomes altered when you are high. Scientists are still trying to understand what this subjective feeling of time distortion is all about. What we do know is that cannabis can make the flow of time seem to stretch out so that just a few minutes can feel like hours.

This feeling of floating in timeless time, free from the mind's usual linear time construction, often elicits the experience of pure bliss . . . a sense of timelessness where the past and the future are almost entirely gone. In this expanded state, even the slightest touch from your lover can seem to last a lifetime and bring truly remarkable pleasure and intimacy.

> **Many people report that they definitely seem to experience more pleasure sexually when they are high. This runs parallel to the general sensory and emotion-heightening effect of weed.**

I began my therapy career in the tradition of the great Austrian sexual scientist Wilhelm Reich, who considered regular weekly orgasms and ever-deepening intimacy to be a prime element of mental and physical health.[14] I no longer practice his specific approach to therapy, nor am I as dogmatic as he was regarding the necessity of overt sexual fulfillment for a satisfying life. There are certainly many other paths. But I do find sexual intimacy to be a healing balm and primary blessing to the human species. And using grass to enhance your sexual experience can have considerable therapeutic value.

People often ask: What about a situation where one person gets high and the other, for whatever reason, doesn't? I've found no research on this, but my personal experience is that it usually works quite well. There is a definite psychological phenomenon, sometimes called the "contact high," in which the person who isn't high picks up the general resonance of the person who is and spontaneously shifts into that mind-set. This happens especially with couples who are familiar with both states.

Traditional Newtonian science would scoff at the idea that we radiate a palpable energetic resonance that can influence another person's mind-set or emotions, but the new quantum physics model of reality indicates that, yes, we are in fact made up not of solid matter but of energetic waves. (For further discussion, see *Quantum Mind: The Edge Between Physics and Physiology,* by Arnold Mindell.) These waves move outward from our physical bodies and engage with the resonant broadcasts of other people. So if one of you is high and the other is not, getting a contact high is a very real possibility.

Many women especially value both types of orgasms – high and not high. The two experiences do seem in several ways different. Questionnaire studies have documented that many women experience more clitoral excitement when they are high, compared with a deeper vaginal experience during a not-high orgasm.

As for men, many report that marijuana enables them to relax and take longer before coming, as they learn from the high experience how to tune in to the more subtle "feminine" softness that makes very slight sensory experience seem to explode in pleasure and expand into timeless time. . . .

On this note, over and over I've heard women praise pot because it helps their male partner slow down and let the sexual encounter delve into unique new realms of intimate relating. Based on the chemical effect of cannabis on sensory sensitivity and time distortion, this makes perfect sense. And of course, this theme has many unique variations depending on your personal sexual preferences.

OUTERCOURSE

Among the more intriguing elements of "sex while high" is the current media buzz about "intercourse" versus "outercourse." Outercourse refers to all the sexually stimulating things a couple can do together without overt penetration and naked intercourse. (It used to be called foreplay.) With the addition of cannabis to the intimate equation, almost invisible orgasm experiences and sexual "skimming" can easily be engaged in if both partners are open to experience the more subtle and even etheric levels of sexual enjoyment.[15]

Danielle, whom we heard from in earlier chapters, gave this report:

Getting high with Jim made me feel sexually like I was fifteen again, very bashful, like I'd hardly ever been kissed before. Jim seemed to feel the same way because after our giggling fit, we just lay there on the rug, breathing together, our bodies touching here and there – and even the slightest movement, the gentlest touch, seemed to set us both afire. He was in a very soft, loving mood, not pushing for intercourse – and I just loved it! I must say, without hardly any overt rubbing at all, time seemed to expand and my orgasm went on and on, almost entirely inwardly. We'd never made love like that before. We were on some new plane together. It seemed as if there were no boundaries at all between us . . . and I felt like every cell in my body somehow came.

I've since learned that a lot of couples sometimes slip effortlessly into this sexual bliss zone, coming together even if they're not having full intercourse.

In fact, when people get really high, to the point that they hardly want to move at all, and they certainly don't want to get the steam up for acrobatic sex, this "outercourse" approach to orgasm can prove to be remarkable – it's soft and subtle, and every chakra fires off, over and over.

SOLITARY HIGH

And now . . . what if you don't at present have a sexual partner? Do you lose out on all this potential pleasurable healing power of sex? I want to speak openly about the traditionally negative but definitely universal occurrence formally called masturbation or self-gratification. For many hundreds of years, both the Catholic and Protestant stance on masturbation insisted that self-gratification was a sin against God and nature. We've come a long way since then, but many people still consider giving themselves sexual pleasure to be somehow negative or demeaning, even though they can't stop from doing it.

Numerous studies have shown that even among married couples, 70 percent of both men and women also masturbate in addition to having sexual intercourse.[16] And this seems perfectly normal, because baby boys often play with their genitals and get erections, and little girls often seem to derive pleasure from masturbatory activity. And health-wise, men who masturbate tend to have a lower incidence of cardiac disease than men who don't.[17]

Wilhelm Reich was right – loads of good things happen when we orgasm regularly. Masturbation is considered a cardiovascular workout, as it gets the heart pounding, the breathing expands, and healthy hormones flush the system to generate relaxation and a sense of overall well-being.

Getting high does often make people feel seriously horny, and even if a self-administered orgasm might not be as deeply engaging or heart-warming as a mutually shared one, the act does generate the same basic aftermath of hormonal flooding through the body. At the peak orgasmic moment, some pretty remarkable things happen throughout the body, whether you're having the experience alone or with a partner. And high or not high, when you get sexually aroused, twin neurohormones called oxytocin and prolactin are secreted in the brain and flow throughout your body to each and every cell, especially to the gonads and breasts and ovaries, bringing a rush of pleasure and sense of well-being.

Endogenous morphine, another strong pleasure elicitor, is also released into your bloodstream during orgasm.[18] It quickly penetrates every cell in your body, generating that remarkable postorgasm experience of total relaxation and bliss. During this bliss phase, the cerebral cortex tempo-rarily experiences less metabolic activity, the buzz of the brain becomes silent, and a bit of true inner peace is naturally experienced.

As I suspect wise folk have known for many moons, marijuana nat-urally expands and enhances this whole-body bliss experience, and in this regard it's definitely a marvelous and valuable herb.

SEX AND SPIRIT

Studies show that beyond the overt sexual rush that accompanies the high experience, there's another dimension that makes this entire dis-cussion especially meaningful: it seems that a great many cannabis users

around the globe discover a special link between sexuality and spirituality when they are high. This naturally causes these people to approach
the cannabis effect with a sense of reverence.

I wrote a book a while back, called *Sex and Spirit: Merging Heart
and Soul in Love,* that explored this sex-and-spirit connection in depth –
but I didn't include cannabis in that discussion. Let me say here that I
find my sexual experiences while I am high of equal value spiritually as
when I'm not high. As long as I stay aware of my breathing when I'm
high, I benefit from deep spiritual insights in much the same way as I
do when I'm not high.

As I get older, the union of sex and spirit continues to get stronger.
As we'll discuss in more depth later, more and more people are discovering that moderate use of pot can extend sexual potency further into
old age, and it can also help make that experience resonate with deeper
spiritual overtones. Also, as we get older, we tend to sink into ingrained
sexual patterns of belief and behavior, rather than staying open to new
experiences and perspectives; cannabis can help with that.

**Cannabis is definitely a positive interrupter of ingrained sexual
behavior because it shifts the mind into exploring new
realms of experience and growth.**

For a balanced discussion, it should perhaps be noted that some
people become addicted to sex, and especially to masturbatory sex, as
a way of regularly stimulating the secretion of natural morphine-based
hormones into the bloodstream. This is a natural way for all human
beings to attain momentary transcendence, but when people retreat into
chronic self-stimulation habits and use marijuana to help enhance this
pattern, to the point that the behavior becomes an acute isolation pattern, then they're probably in need of helpful therapy.

But for most people with or without a sexual partner, using marijuana to enhance sexual stimulation and even perhaps to tap a bit of
spiritual revelation seems both natural and healthy.

We're always being challenged to be 100 percent human and
earthly and rooted in our natural biological presence, while
at the same time we aspire to transcend everyday mortal
consciousness and find eternal oneness in spiritual
awakening. How can we do both?

I often repeat the following story, but it's always relevant because it expresses a possible resolution to the paradox of being 100 percent human and 100 percent divine: When I was in my twenties, I studied for four years with a philosopher in San Francisco named Alan Watts, a flawed but wonderful and inspiring teacher and spiritual pioneer who embraced marijuana and psychedelics as helpmates on the spiritual path.[19] He said over and over that we must see ourselves and everyone else as 100 percent human and *also* 100 percent divine – and in order to do so, we must expand our definition of reality to include two 100 percent truths.

The traditional yin-yang symbol of a circle with an S drawn inside it, dividing the circle into two equal parts within the greater encircling whole, expresses this leap into a 200 percent reality. Our entire universe operates as a dualistic system, but for me, a greater unifying force and consciousness beyond the seeming duality must exist to hold the entire physical universe together.

Nowhere is this a more obvious truth than in sexual intercourse. When we become sexually aroused, we regress into raw animal urges and behavior, while at the same time, during orgasm, we often experience total transcendence of normal consciousness and feel as if we've entered the kingdom of Eros – Heaven. Yes, scientists can partly explain the orgasm/bliss phenomenon through biochemical models, and yet scientists cannot explain what consciousness itself is.

When we get high, often we encounter deep spiritual ideas that seem to make perfect sense to our high perspective of reality. This expansive sense of inquiry into the deeper nature of the universe seems to naturally accompany the cannabis buzz.[20] And as one well-known scientist who openly lauded marijuana's power to stimulate scientific and spiritual insight, Carl Sagan, concluded in his later years, "Science is not only compatible with spirituality; it is a profound source of spirituality."

We live in a dualistic three-dimensional physical world in our mortal bodies – but our minds can sometimes encounter a nondual quality of consciousness that totally transcends physical reality.

To the extent that cannabis and sexual relating together can help us experience a spiritual awakening, we're very lucky that earthly creation has somehow included the cannabis plant, and that humans finally mastered fire and discovered that if we smoke it (or cook it and ingest the herb), we can become temporarily lifted into spiritual realms of being.

LOSING IN ORDER TO GAIN

As we've been exploring, making love is all about temporarily letting go of the past and future and instead focusing entirely on the sensory present moment. For a brief time, your usual adult fixation on what just happened to you and what might happen in the near future gets mostly lost. Instead, you surrender this function of the mind and become acutely focused on all the present-moment sensory events flooding into your brain.

This is definitely a major mind-set shift – and it makes sexual relating come alive! The marijuana muse leads us off away from our minds and reawakens an early-childhood sense of total engagement with our overt bodily presence. Young children tend to experience the world as constantly new and exciting; everything seems worth exploring and learning about. Because youthful minds aren't yet stuffed with limiting attitudes and beliefs, little kids are naturally very much in the present moment rather than mired in memories about the past or worries about the future.

Marijuana seems to temporarily induce or reintroduce a similar youthful experience of suddenly seeing everything as fresh and new – as if for the first time.

This seems to be what happens with sexual relating when we are high. THC gently forces us to relinquish all judgmental comparisons and associations with past lovemaking experiences. By totally indulging in the pleasure of the moment, we're able to discover the newness in each moment.

The associative function of the mind is, of course, a truly remarkable and valuable process. It enables us to plot and plan and judge and react to the present moment – but it also separates us from directly experiencing and appreciating the ongoing pleasure of the now. When everything we encounter instantly reminds us of something we've encountered before, there's very little freshness or adventure attached to our present-moment encounters. When they are not high, many people are unconsciously stuck in this pattern while making love. Then, when they get high, it all changes.

The cannabis muse helps us to once again look at a flower and experience the pure multisensory presence of that flower.

This shift in mind-set is invaluable when you are making love, particularly if you've made love to this person a dozen, a hundred, or even thousands of times before, and all your sensory inputs in the present moment remind you instantly of almost identical inputs you've had in the past. I'm not saying that we need marijuana to stay satisfied and eager when making love for the thousandth time with the same partner – but it can surely help.

POSTORGASM BLISS

I might mention a final benefit from combining marijuana and sex: the expanded depth of experience that can last for quite some time after orgasm. The cannabis effect will often continue to stretch out your sense of time or even generate a sense of timelessness as the aftermath of orgasm flushes your whole body with a cacophony of pleasure hormones.

There's nothing quite like relaxing and indulging fully as every cell in your body receives a chemical hit of ecstasy and release.

Many couples report that their deepest experiences of intimacy happen during this quiet, motionless ecstatic phase when they're both sated and yet still together in their hearts, just breathing and staying in touch with their feelings. Sharing space . . . and love.

CONSCIOUS SEXUAL PLEASURE

To sum up this chapter, let's consider our universal sexual predicament: most people don't want to be told how to make love. But at the same time, when making love, we tend to get continually caught up in so many thoughts, memories, associations, and future projections that lovemaking sometimes seems quite robotic and overly predictable. Our encounters are not as fun and moving as they could be because we're being dominated by the mind rather than the body. No sexual situation can be satisfying or uplifting when the two people involved are busy in their minds trying to figure out what to do next, or are habitually judging what's happening based on previous encounters, or are imagining being with someone else . . . and so on and so forth.

We need to somehow break free from all our ingrained mental-sexual habits and quiet our mind for a while so that we can become more spontaneous in our erotic lives.

Whether you are high or not, erotic heart-to-heart fulfillment begins and hopefully also ends by tuning in to your own body and at the same time focusing on your partner's living, breathing presence.

As we've seen, the trick is to focus on just being together, breathing together, letting everything drop down to a silent shared still point. This is most easily accomplished by the primal act of letting go of all ego control. Here's a guided experience that lets you experience inner quiet, right at the very bottom of your exhalations (you can also listen to the audio on the High Together app):

Get comfortable . . . and choose to do absolutely nothing for a few minutes – just let your next inhalations and exhalations come and go . . . and stop and start . . . with zero effort. Trust the life force to continue breathing for you as you surrender to pure stillness deep inside.

Now, on your next breath, pause for a moment at the bottom of your exhalation . . . then let your next inhalation come rushing in until you're full . . . and now exhale completely again . . . and at the bottom, experience being entirely empty of everything – air, thoughts, feelings, intentions, hungers.

Now allow your next inhalation to come rushing in, without your making it happen in any way . . . continue with your next exhalation to the bottom . . . and right at that zero point, experience pure peace and quiet . . . and continue breathing freely. . . .

At some point, your body might begin to feel a slight hint of a delicious stretch that's forming all on its own. Breathe and surrender to this urge to stretch . . . and feel all the thousands of sensations rushing to your brain as you move freely until you're thoroughly satisfied. . . .

NINE

Sharing New Creative Insights

*Believing innocently in yourself
and trusting your natural responses,
you can move into the unknown
with nothing to fear.*

*You can look beyond the obvious
to what is hidden and obscure
and in total trust awaken
all the unlimited possibilities
you hold within yourself.*

*And when you're together and
high with a trusted companion,
you can combine your two
creative urges into one
unique expression of clarity,
simplicity, and pure abandon!*

As we're seeing, there's a fairly predictable progression to the cannabis high. The first ten to twenty minutes, even the first hour, can be quite intense if you used a high-THC strain of cannabis. Even moderate psychedelic experiences can happen, along with sexual relating. However, what happens after that first wild rush is of equal importance. Now the psychic dust settles and overt pleasure evolves into more intuitive and even mystic realms of encounter.

Successful couples in general share not only intellectual, sexual, and sensation aspects of relating. They also share the more invisible dimensions of growing emotionally and creating a meaningful life together. There's great fulfillment in discovering a common life purpose, in sharing a creative project, or in enjoying intuitive philosophical or religious bonding, not to mention the magic of two hearts and minds and bodies feeling energetically merged. When two lives are pulsing to the same core rhythm . . . life is good.

Taking time to just relax together, perhaps in bed, in easy chairs, or out strolling together through nature, is definitely an important "denouement" phase of cannabis intimacy.

As you ease up into the latter stages of a shared high, you're free to choose to focus attention mutually on whatever theme, process, or creative expression you find of value. Together, you might read from the work of a favorite poet or spiritual teaching, enjoy music (or make music!), cook, share an artistic experience, or focus on a particular project or opportunity. This creative expression can happen spontaneously, but a little planning just ahead of the high experience can help you guide and enhance the process.

THE FREE TIME DILEMMA

The importance of free, open, undisturbed time is often overlooked or ignored in our speedy contemporary society, where every minute tends to get stuffed full of urgent activity. Time-management studies show that most people reserve almost no free time in their daily schedules – and this, in my opinion, is one of the primary killers of enduring relationships. Love needs open time and devoted shared attention in order to grow and evolve.

When two people come together to nurture a lasting deep friendship of any kind, they do need to commit to regularly creating free time when they can pause and just be together. Within this free time, two people can allow their separate souls and personalities, their emotions and intentions, to relax and discover common ground. This free time experience nurtures the shared sense of peace and fulfillment in a relationship. Pausing like this is, of course, a bit risky; who knows what we might discover when we stop and quietly share space and time with our partner?

This is the time when true spiritual intercourse has room to happen. It's where the muse of cannabis can reveal truly new pathways for us to walk together.

There are many variations on this "beyond the buzz" free time theme. What's important is choosing to create open time within which to enjoy each other's company and interests. Love requires us to be open to discovering newness with someone – and the newness can emerge only when there's time and a safe space within which it can manifest.

Let's experiment with this for a few moments. After reading this section, close your eyes, if you want to, and tune in to your breathing and whole-body presence . . . and imagine that you're with your loved one, high and relaxing together.

Be aware of your own natural bubble of awareness as your senses expand to fill your environment. Now begin to notice how your own bubble of awareness can expand to include your partner and yourself in a larger sphere of awareness.

Breathe into this expansive feeling . . . let your hearts sing in harmony with the pure pleasure of being together, with no pressing demands on your time . . . and now set your imagination free to see what the two of you might spontaneously flow into experiencing together. . . .

ALONE TOGETHER

Although there's often a natural flow to the sequence of what happens when a couple gets high together, I also want to keep saying that no two couples are the same, and no two high experiences are the same. Often you and your partner will find your personal experience running parallel with the flow of the seven dimensions I'm outlining in this book. But at any time, your experience can veer off into quite unexpected realms and patterns.

For instance, even though you might have set your mutual intention to spend a couple of hours together while high, sometimes you'll find that you naturally want to go off and do something solo, on your own – and you gracefully express your desire and then act on it.

> **If you agree beforehand that this might happen and that it's perfectly okay, then you can go spend time alone and not feel guilty.**

This might seem overly obvious, but I've found that all too often, if this theme is not expressed clearly and openly, there can arise misunderstandings and hurt feelings. So do talk through this "going solo" theme together before getting high. We talked earlier about how balance is so important in many aspects of a relationship, and nowhere is it more important than in this foundational balance of time spent together and time spent alone.

Especially when we are high, we can seriously fry our conversational synapses and just plain run dry of relating energy. We saw how it helps to agree to use sign language as a sign that you've had enough talking; you simply raise your hand, palm out, to indicate that you want to drop out of a conversation. This allows you to take a breather and recharge your conversational batteries. Sometimes you'll want more than just a quick break; you'll feel the urge to go off and do something utterly alone for a while.

When I lived in San Luis Obispo, I worked with a couple who

almost broke up over this very point. Ruth was an artist by profession, and Kenny was the manager of a local ranch. He was fairly gregarious and enjoyed long conversations about philosophy and politics and such, while Ruth was more of an introvert who cherished both her shared life and her solitary life. When they got high together, she'd often suddenly leave him all alone while she went into her studio with a great new creative idea. Kenny would get upset and drive off in his pickup to party with some friends without her.

She came to me because she thought Kenny wasn't interested in her anymore, but she didn't know why. When I got them together to talk things through, it didn't take much detective work to identify the communication problem. He actually thought that *she* wasn't interested in *him* any longer because she kept leaving him halfway through a deep conversation and retreating into her private space.

The solution was obviously a sharing of their opposite perspectives so that they realized what was actually happening, rather than projecting assumptions onto each other. He had no idea that when the creative muse came and tapped her on the shoulder, she compulsively (and eagerly) had to respond and go off alone to grab her paintbrush. And he finally confessed that, yeah, almost every day he had the urge to retreat, to go off on his horse or Jeep way out to the back of the ranch and spend some time alone.

Once they understood each other's need for solitary space, everything relaxed between them. They very much valued their high time together as a couple on a regular basis, two or three times a week, but they also realized that they shared the need for solo time.

So whether you need just five minutes or much longer to go off and do your own solitary thing, be transparent about your need. Even in the best of relationships, solitary time is essential. This is when you reflect, when you commune with your own inner realms of being, when you let the social air clear and regain your own individual center. If you don't grant yourself the freedom to do this when you need it, your relationship is going to suffer.

You'll also want to consider that even when you're alone and away from your partner, there's a sense in which you remain connected. That's what a relationship is all about – you feel together in your hearts even when you're physically distant. In fact, there are times when you might feel most deeply your oneness with your partner when you're distant! It's true, and quite possible; quantum science, as I mentioned earlier, is busy proving that there's a nonmaterial energetic connection between two people that transcends space and time.

Science hasn't fully detailed it yet, but I'm convinced from personal experience as well as entanglement research that a subtle energetic resonance happens between two bodies, minds, hearts, and souls that love each other, no matter what the distance.

THE CREATIVE MUSE

Whether you're creating something with your partner or doing your own separate thing, marijuana does often seem to boost creativity.[1] A great many artists, authors, musicians, and other innovators claim to have used cannabis as a way to awaken their creative juices. This list includes Charles Baudelaire and George Carlin, Paul McCartney and Jack Nicholson, William Shakespeare and Louis Armstrong, Carl Sagan and Norman Mailer, Brian Wilson and Matthew McConaughey, Whoopi Goldberg and Sarah Silverman, Snoop Dogg and Bill Mayer, and Keith Richards and Willie Nelson.[2]

Does using cannabis actually spur creativity, and how can this effect be managed to your best advantage? According to a 2011 study reported in *Psychology Today,* cognitive scientists concluded that "a drug-induced altered state of mind with cannabis may indeed lead to breaking free from ordinary thinking and associations, thereby, increasing the likelihood of generating novel ideas or associations."[3] Indeed, fMRI experiments show that marijuana often increases activity in the prefrontal lobes of the brain, indicating that the associative process of the mind is being stimulated.

Marijuana also tends to exaggerate emotions and provoke unexpected associations and fresh thoughts. Creativity depends on our ability to access and record unusual links between different ideas.[4] When we're high, we do tend to relax our mental habits and inhibitions that limit free-roaming associations. Scientifically, this can be explained by cannabis's stimulating dopamine release in the mesolimbic pathway, which includes the frontal cortex.

Cannabis often seems to help us connect two or more different ideas or imaginations in new ways. When the effects of pot take over, our judgmental function that inhibits new ideas and imaginations temporarily eases up, and we're able to entertain mental risks and leaps that lead us into exploring new creative possibilities. Also, when we're not worried about results and focus more fully on the present moment, we enter a state where we're more playful – and this is a great boost to creativity.[5]

We have already seen that marijuana helps us regress into child-like patterns of free play and pure pleasure, and this state is optimal for waking up creative ideas and expressions. When the imagination is set free, creativity flowers. Also, weed helps us focus intensely on one thing to the exclusion of all else, which is another feature of creativity. Here's a list of positives regarding pot and creativity:

- Cannabis enhances our ability to focus our attention powerfully on one particular intent or creative act.
- Episodic memory retrieval is enhanced, meaning that we are better able to vividly recall a particular event, empowering a deeper exploration of that event or related themes.
- Marijuana encourages inward reflection and introspection, so that we are better able to assess our feelings and ideas, contemplate in depth, and sometimes discover something truly new to express in music, art, philosophy, and so forth.

- Using pot can improve our pattern recognition, which is one of the most important aspects of creativity. This means that we can recognize new patterns and use those new patterns to create unexpected breakthroughs in design, organization, and certainly music and art.
- Cannabis boosts our ability to make associative connections. In this way, for example, writers and speakers can make new connections between words and concepts and thus express themselves with deeper meaning and unique wording. When we are able to see similarities in seemingly disparate concepts and patterns, truly new ideas can spring to life.
- Marijuana definitely stimulates blood flow into the frontal lobe of the brain, which is thought to be the seat of creativity.[6]

Creativity involves integrating a unique combination of conceptual thinking, vivid imagination, focused memory, and uninhibited reflection. Sometimes this process manifests as a new idea or pattern; at other times, it becomes a musical, story-telling, culinary, or other artistic expression.

> The sky's the limit with creativity; in any area of interest
> or profession, there's always room and need
> for new ideas and inspirations.

And how does this apply to you and your partner when you're high? Right at the beginning of a shared cannabis adventure, we saw that a reduction in inhibition can lead to spontaneous chattering, which can lead to creative brainstorming, breakthroughs, and resolutions of shared problems. But creativity doesn't have to be turned into anything tangible – it's great fun to just explode with great ideas and imaginations, even if nothing comes of the creative flow.

As a couple, it's important to honor the marijuana muse when it provokes intense creative urges. At any moment, a powerful urge to create something may hit one of you. It's important to discuss this possibility ahead of time so that the other person can recognize what's happening and set the other immediately free to go off and create.

Very often you'll be creatively struck with new ideas and imaginations that you can work on together. This is one of the great pleasures of being high with someone who lets you be fully uninhibited – who knows what will happen!

Let's remember that being creative doesn't mean that other people have to value your creativity. There's no need to achieve celebrity status or to create some publicly lauded masterpiece.

It can mean that you suddenly have a great idea for how to plant your summer garden this year; it can mean that you solve the problem of what to cook for a family dinner the next evening; it can mean suddenly putting two and two together and resolving a conflict you've had all your life with your big brother; it can mean realizing anything at all that feels like a breakthrough or a new way of seeing things. That's creativity!

THE TRIANGLE ELEMENT

In the opposite direction of solitary creative retreat, sometimes you and your partner, rather than feeling the urge to go solo, might enjoy bringing another person into your shared bubble, temporarily creating a triangle relationship among the three of you. If you're more adventuresome than I am, this might include a sexual dimension. But usually the erotic element is put aside when a third person comes into your high bubble.

You might choose to get high as a threesome and move through whichever of the seven dimensions that we've discussed naturally emerge. Or perhaps a friend will drop by and join you after you've already been high for an hour or so, and the three of you will pick up wherever you might be in that flow of phases. With a third person in the mix, often the conversational aspect dominates, but this doesn't have to be the case.

If your third person understands the principles of this book and program, you can all explore any dimension of a shared high.

Three people relating is quite different from two people relating. In a three-way conversation, usually one person talks while holding eye contact with a second person, while the third person simply listens. You might want to notice this dynamic the next time you're in a three-way conversation. Especially when you're all high, you'll notice that if you're the "third person out" in a conversation, you have a lot of freedom to get centered, regain awareness of your breathing, drop down into your heartful emotions, and then return to active participation in the conversation in a refreshed spirit.

This three-person conversational dynamic sometimes becomes a challenge when you are all high because with three people all sharing one idea or focus, the triangle effect usually makes the relating less intimate.

So there can be a big trade-off when your high experience goes from two to three people. If you add several more people, the dynamic shifts again. More intimacy is lost, but you gain the feeling of belonging to a group. Whether or not this is something you want is up to you and your partner. Honestly sharing your current social and intimate needs helps greatly in making the best decision.

INTIMATE BUT ALSO INCLUSIVE

The mating instinct is one of the most powerful human drives. If you're in a relationship with another person, you probably moved through the eight standard stages of the human mating instinct: First you viewed each other from a distance, perhaps at work, at a social gathering, or while you were out walking the dog. Then came the "pickup" stage, in which you moved toward each other and tentatively made your introductions. One way or another, this was followed by the "chatter" stage, when you used casual discourse to explore whether you were similar enough to risk getting closer. Then at some point, real intimacy sparked and the "bodily contact" stage began. This was followed by the "cuddling" stage, which is often a regression to cozy infancy urges. Then came the sixth stage of exploring the feeling of being a couple – walking hand in hand, touching vulnerable parts of the body, and so forth. The seventh stage brought you to full sexual intimacy, and the eighth stage fulfilled the flow toward union with mutual dedication to each other as a bonded pair.

You might notice that you often move through all or at least most of these stages each time you get high together as a couple. You get caught glancing into each other's eyes deeply . . . then you chatter together . . . perhaps you touch tentatively and then cuddle and enjoy the rush of mutual attraction . . . and this might be followed by foreplay and perhaps full sexual union.

As a couple, you explore together what your coupling actually is going to mature into. Will you have children? Will you share a home? Will you do a business as a duo team? Will you travel and discover the world? One way or another, you form a dyad bond, a mate relationship, an exclusive commitment of one sort or another for whatever time duration comes naturally. And many couples leave it at that – they retreat into their dyad cocoon and never come out.

In moderation, this is fine and essential for families to come into being and parenting to be successful. But it's all too easy to bond with your intimate partner and exclude everyone else from your circle. Life involves more than just one other person. So while you are high, you might want to explore together whether you want to be more inclusive in your social circle and allow other people into your shared bubble.

> **Being inclusive means trusting and sharing. It's the opposite of being selfish with the person you love. As spiritual teachers often say, real love means setting your lover free. And this requires a lot of confidence and inner strength.**

When you're high and relaxing into the later phases of a shared experience, you might want to reflect on whether you actually love your partner enough to set them free to follow their own personal needs and yearnings. How secure are you in your relationship? When you ask such questions while you are high, you might find new insights flowing, new feelings emerging, and new possibilities arising.

NEW ONE-LINERS

As mentioned earlier, we all got programmed as kids with a host of negative one-liners and subconscious judgmental attitudes. Recently there's been a resurgence of self-help programs focused on this topic of breaking free from hidden verbal reflexes and childhood beliefs that generate blame, hostility, low self-esteem, and so forth. This de-beliefing process can actually transform someone's life.

In my therapy work, I would often use the muse of marijuana to help clients grow rapidly into a brighter and more realistic attitude about themselves and the world. You can tap into this helpful process when you are high together with your partner to help each other transcend debilitating beliefs that simply don't serve you anymore.

I'm not suggesting that you take all your old beliefs out back and shoot them (as my cowboy granddad would have said). Many of your ingrained attitudes and subconscious beliefs are positive, realistic, and vital to living a good life. But I've never met anyone who didn't have at least a few old reflexive one-liners in need of culling.

For easy and instant entry into this de-beliefing process while high together, you and your partner can play a game that's both fun and highly productive – and often revealing and liberating. You can play this game either when you are first getting high and going through a conversation buzz, or during the later phase when you're relaxing together, as described in this chapter. You may want to have a notepad or big piece of paper at hand so you can jot down your responses to the questions. Just get comfortable, and take turns writing down whatever pops into mind when you each ask yourself the following:

What's an old belief that I'd like to get rid of?

At first just play lightly with this, saying the most obvious one-liners that most people secretly harbor, such as "I'm no good," "Nobody likes me," "Nothing ever works out right," or "Life is boring." Other popular one-liners include "I'm too dumb," "You can't trust strangers," and "I'll never get ahead." It's remarkable how many of us have such self-demeaning one-liners lurking in the shadows of our subconscious minds, continually polluting our attitudes and expectations.

Most of us also carry unspoken but still-lurking prejudicial one-liners against people and groups that our parents were prejudiced against, including racial minorities and people of different religious faiths, political parties, or even colleges and nearby towns. We may believe, "I hate the Dodgers," "That type of person is dangerous," "Catholics are lazy," and so forth. Often I've found that even people who think they're free of prejudice have buried one-liners that undermine their relating. Unearthing and letting go of these unconscious prejudices can actively brighten our society.

When you play this game with your partner while you are high, be sure not to feel guilty or accusing when either of you admit to having a really horrible negative one-liner, no matter how unfair or demeaning it might be. The goal here isn't to judge; it's to identify and then consciously let go of all your negative one-liner beliefs that otherwise hold you back in life.

So just go ahead, brainstorm, and come up with as many of your negative one-liner beliefs and attitudes as you can think of. You'll find that being high makes it relatively easy for hidden one-liners to pop into mind. Share them with your partner, write them down, and then do this.

After you write down a negative one-liner, also write down its exact opposite – the positive one-liner that you'd prefer to install in your subconscious to take the place of the negative one. Be sure to write down the exact opposite. For instance:

I'll never get ahead > I'm making good progress
Nobody likes me > I feel well loved
Everybody's a crook > People are trustworthy
I'm a terrible person > I'm a good person
I'm cursed > I'm blessed
Life sucks > Things are pretty good these days
I give up > I'm winning
I hate myself > I love who I am
This is hopeless > Things will work out
I won't do it > Okay, I'll do it
You're mean > I accept how you are
I reject my past > I honor my ancestors
I feel dead > I feel alive
I'll never make it > I've got it made
I won't bow down > I'm willing to surrender
Nobody listens to me > Thank you for listening
I don't know what's going on > I understand all this
I miss the past > I'm enjoying the present moment

Play this game by writing down your paired list of one-liners, and then each of you can read down your list, saying first a rejection of the negative: "It's not true that I'll never get ahead. I now let go of that attitude forever." You might want to envision writing your negative one-liner on a piece of paper and then throwing that paper into a fire and watching it burn up into nothingness. Or you can actually do this burning physically with paper and lighter. Gone for good!

Then you'll want to clearly state out loud the positive one-liner that you want to actively reprogram your subconscious mind with – for instance, "I'm making good progress!" What's important is to say out loud to your partner and the universe the negation of the negative and then the declaration of the positive, so that the key elicitor words and ideas will penetrate deeply into your subconscious realms.

I recommend that you return to your list and restate your positive one-liners several times over the following days, so that you strongly imprint in your mind a new positive stance in life. Also, try doing this process while high, and then again while not high, and see the difference in impact.

Notice that with each dual entry, you are free to choose which you want – the negative or positive. Be honest with yourself because some of the negative one-liners might represent how you still feel, and you'll want to nonjudgmentally recognize and honor the fact that right now, you're still caught in this negative stance. As you return to this negative one-liner often, you'll naturally begin to let go of it, I assure you. And the muse of cannabis seems to exert a special healing power to help in this de-beliefing process. For more guidance with this process, and to access additional "what to do while high together" programs, feel free to visit the Mindfully High website.

TEN

Mutual Awakening

What can I say . . .
a leaf floating
fluttering
to the ground
and then settling
satisfied.

For it has been a day
of timeless time
floating weightless
through the universe
of my mind.

And now
nowhere to go
nothing to do
all things possible.

This seventh and usually final dimension of a couple's high experience is often forgotten entirely, and it might seem quite different from everything we've discussed before, but this final phase may also be the most important of all. As you gently begin to come down from the early rush of your mutual marijuana high, you'll both probably find that there often comes a moment when time seems to stand still, and it seems that there's nothing left to do or say or feel or explore.

Right at this moment, when you're with your partner but not necessarily relating in any overt way, a host of new shared experiences can suddenly and softly emerge.

Why? Because finally both of you have finished doing everything you wanted to; you have no active intent or energy charge pushing you to do anything at all. Finally, you're just being together, in the deeper sense of the word.

THC and CBD stay in your bloodstream not just for minutes or even hours, but for days after you partake.[1] So there's a long denouement, or aftermath phase, that you'll feel for at least a few hours after you partake. If you smoke or vape or drop, the first hour after ingesting is the "rush time," and then the second hour is usually the kickback post-rush phase. It's mellow and subtle, but it's also often the most rewarding for couples because you share what's often felt as a spiritually imbued state of pure being.

TRIPPING TOGETHER

Ever since the 1960s, people have talked about "tripping" while using marijuana or a psychedelic. A major difference between weed and classic psychedelics such as LSD is that with weed you have some choice in how deeply you're going to take off into the wild blue yonder, whereas with psychedelics, you're catapulted into tripping zones whether you like it or not. With marijuana, often you'll start to feel as if you're floating, as though you've transcended space and time – and this is certainly a quality of tripping. But as we mentioned earlier, usually you won't hallucinate with cannabis unless you take a really big dose.[2]

Tripping on weed is determined primarily by whether you ask for

such an experience by relaxing on an easy chair, sofa, or bed and surrendering for a period of time to utterly letting go and looking inward
for new experience. You could instead focus outward to your five senses
and trip out on that stimulation, but this seventh dimension of a shared
cannabis trip usually involves closing your eyes and focusing on whatever naturally springs to heart and mind deep within you.

Many people love to trip out with music. Music is truly magical;
it's been used for tripping in religious ceremonial practices all over the
world for thousands of years. And cannabis has a definite effect on how
we hear music. One study of THC showed "a constant EEG correlate
of temporarily intensified attention while high, resulting in an altered
music perception, hyperfocusing on acoustic space and broadened
insight into the 'space between the notes.' In sum, THC has a measur-
able influence on cerebral music processing, and seems to temporarily
enhance acoustic perception."[3]

Music often includes reflective lyrics that can stimulate deep intuitive thought and realization. Before getting high, you'll probably want
to develop your own playlist of music that suits you and your partner
best. Be quite choosy; you'll want music that augments your experience,
rather than disturbing it. There are various playlists for tripping that
you can find online; most are designed for use with psychedelics, but
they are also quite good for cannabis journeys.[4]

One of the best ways to go deeply into a weed trip is to combine
very good relaxing music with an ongoing awareness of your breathing. You'll quickly entrain your breathing rhythm with the rhythm
of the music, and this will bring you into a whole-body experience
that taps into your inner sense of embodiment. And as you do this,
you'll often experience a floating sensation that will carry you off
into your own unique realms of interior exploration. If you want further instruction on cannabis and embodiment meditations, a friend
of mine from way back in college, Will Johnson, has written a great
book on the subject, *Cannabis in Spiritual Practice: The Ecstasy of
Shiva, the Calm of Buddha.*

When you and your partner listen together to music while you
are both high, often there emerges a shared sense of oneness
and resonant union; it can't as yet be proven scientifically
but is certainly experienced intimately.

When you listen to music, your ears and also your skin are touched directly by the sound vibrations coming to you through the air – and as we saw earlier, the skin is a remarkable sense organ. The tiny hairs that cover your skin vibrate with the music, the pulse of the music itself seems to penetrate the skin, and cannabis, with its expansion of our sensory abilities, accentuates the entire experience. People who are high often experience goosebumps or chills – a frisson – while listening to moving music; it can feel like a "skin orgasm" of deep intensity.[5] Feeling this whole-body skin orgasm together with your partner is quite a remarkable experience.

When you listen to music, sometimes your breathing syncs up with the beat. Sometimes you find yourself mouthing the words or responding to music with your own subtle harmonies; sometimes you surrender to the "sing-along" reflex. Muscles throughout your body will pulse to the music. Sharing this pleasure with your partner – feeling your bodies pulse in time to the music together – is an intimate experience and readily available!

Tripping in silence is equally valuable. Music naturally evokes and shapes an emotional response in listeners. When you turn off the music and enjoy silence together, your trip can deepen because it's not being limited by the emotional conditioning or lyrics of the music.

Many couples like to go back and forth, maybe every ten
minutes or so, between listening to a few mutually enjoyable
tunes and then turning off the music and sharing silence.

In this silence, meditation becomes a natural quality of shared consciousness. Suddenly there's peace and quiet. There is nothing you have to pay attention to; there's just you and your partner breathing within the space you share. Cannabis helps you tune in to the reality that the very air has substance, and that substance (as quantum scientists insist) connects you quite intimately, even across a room. The air your friend breathed a moment ago is now flowing into your own lungs – that's intimate!

> Breathing into shared space also involves taking in the exact same elements that have been flowing around in the Earth's atmosphere literally since the beginnings of life on this Earth.

I remember a long time ago, during a high session, when I suddenly put two and two together and remembered a science course where I was taught that the very same oxygen-forming atoms that Jesus and Buddha and Lao-tzu breathed are still around – and being breathed by us right now. Wow.

That's the level of realization that can come while we are tripping. We have loads of information in our brains, and with cannabis we will suddenly see the connection between two disparate things, making a new association and realization. Many people who're devoted to marijuana consider this to be the prime positive effect of the herb. Each of us has collected a lifetime's worth of memories, experiences, imaginations, ideas, and so forth, and the muse of cannabis loves to explore this vast inner storehouse to discover unique associative flashes.

SUCCESSFUL DISTANCING

We talked earlier about the necessity of regularly retreating from interacting with your partner while you are high. This freedom to temporarily retreat back into your own separate presence is especially important during the final phase of a shared high. I wrote a book a while ago for the German market called *Successful Distancing,* that examines how sustainable relationships pulsate from a state of being very close to then being quite apart . . . and then naturally coming back close together again, throughout the day, the week, the month, and so on.

> This ongoing "close-distant-close" pulsation is key because
> otherwise, with no alone time, even if you love each other
> deeply, you'll tend to emotionally suffocate each other.

It's great to come very close together when you first get high, but it's also liberating to learn to give your partner complete freedom, at every stage of the high experience, to retreat from engagement and focus entirely within. As mentioned earlier, it's important that you and your partner openly discuss and nurture this spontaneous dyad pulsation pattern that will occur while you are high so that you don't feel rejected when the other temporarily lets go of relating – which naturally happens often in the denouement phase.

This idea of temporary "distancing" might seem a bit strange at first, but you'll soon discover that the more time you spend in a solitary phase of the couples pulsation, the more you'll have to share when you come together again. Balance is all. It's a bit like hitting the "refresh" button when a web page has become sluggish; you retreat into an interior meditation for a few minutes . . . and then enjoy a recharged engagement when you tune in to your partner again.

HIGH MEDITATION

Coming down gently from a shared high – easing up and enjoying the feeling of being satisfied, complete, and content – is an optimum time to explore meditating together. This inner focus can be a purely secular meditation or any traditional meditation/prayer format. On the Mindfully High website, you'll find several different types of guided audio meditations to explore, depending on your religious or philosophical preferences. What's key is consciously creating free time where you can just relax, tune in to inner realms of discovery, and see what happens.

Meditation, in essence, is simple: it involves being still and quiet, gently calming your breathing and your mind, and focusing your full attention toward feeling and accepting the wholeness of your present-moment inner experience.

Usually meditation is seen as an internal solitary process, but if you wish, you can easily include the presence of your partner in your meditation bubble.

It seems that whatever we do in life, there's one overriding factor that determines our experience: whether we're staying aware of our own inner center of being, or we're lost in the sensations, thoughts, and activities of the outside world. If you want to experience a meditative sense of union with your partner while meditating, first you'll need to focus toward and merge with your own inner center; only then can you expand your awareness bubble from the center of your personal being outward to merge with your partner's bubble.

When both of you agree on this dynamic, you can choose to explore it deeply together in the denouement phase of your shared highs. It takes a bit of practice to master the process, so here's some simple guidance (turn to the High Together app if you prefer the audio guide):

Get comfortable . . . stretch a bit if you want to . . . tune in to your breathing, feeling the air flowing effortlessly in and out.

Now expand your awareness from your effortless breaths coming and going to include your whole-body presence . . . be aware of your own presence from the inside out . . . now open your awareness to the feelings you find in your heart . . . breathe into these feelings without judging or trying to change them.

Let every new breath continue to expand your bubble of awareness effortlessly all around your physical body . . . enjoy your full human presence and practice just "being." . . .

Now begin to imagine that your loved one is beside you in the room, breathing the same air that you are breathing right now . . . and experience your partner's bubble and your bubble merging and resonating in harmony together . . . effortlessly and joyfully, experience your two personal bubbles expanding to become one shared bubble!

Enjoy this shared experience . . . let it take you where it will right now . . . and end this meditation whenever you feel ready. . . .

~~~~~~

You can also do formal traditional Buddhist Vipassana meditation. Here's the basic flow:

~~~~~~

Sit quietly for twenty minutes or so each day. Stay aware of the air flowing in and out of your nose . . . and observe the habitual functioning of your mind, your thoughts, imaginations, and all the rest, without getting attached or involved in that habitual mental and emotional activity.

Give yourself permission to let go of your ego-based aware-ness, and instead be the silent witness to what's happening in your mind and body. Feel your deeper awareness gently disen-gage from all your senses, thoughts, and bodily reactions . . . let yourself experience a few moments of perfect inner calm and balance . . . just breathe into the eternal present moment flowing through you. . . .

~~~~~~

The benefits of doing this type of meditation regularly are won-derful, especially if you stick with it for a month or two. And you can always choose to share this sort of meditation with your partner while you're high together. In fact, the muse of marijuana will often lead you spontaneously in this direction. All you need to do is open up and go along with the natural flow into inner peace, oneness, and mutual joy.

LUCID DREAMING

I want to include here at least a short mention of what's often called lucid dreaming, which refers to our natural ability to enter into a dream state while also staying aware that we're dreaming, and to sometimes consciously guide the dream experience.[6] Along with being a great way to end a high experience, lucid dreaming is quite an effective therapeutic tool, and it has recently become almost a national fad – but it actually has its roots way back in ancient history.

In Tibetan yogic practice, many spiritual masters practiced "dream yoga"[7] to help awaken various meditative states.[8] In Buddhist tradition, all of existence was seen as a dream state, and dream yoga was an effective way to explore the nature of existence. Similar to current quantum physics insights showing that all matter is in reality energetic and not physical, the Hindu and Buddhist yogic view considered lucid dream experiences to be equally real to everyday waking experiences. Likewise, in early Greek writings, both Aristotle and Galen of Pergamon discussed the value of lucid dreaming. And a few hundred years later, Saint Augustine wrote about the process and value of lucid dreaming related to the Christian tradition.

Numerous philosophers during the Age of Enlightenment talked about conscious guided dreaming, and of course Sigmund Freud dealt in depth with the therapeutic power of dream states, as did Carl Jung in a more spiritual bent. But it wasn't until 1913 that a Dutch psychiatrist named Frederik van Eeden coined the term "lucid dreaming." Because we all dream, all cultures seem to have their own version of lucid dreaming, dream interpretation, and guided visionary experience.

Even before written history, it seems that shamanic masters regularly mixed dreaming and the ceremonial use of psychotropic substances. Carlos Castaneda explored in depth the Yaqui Indian use of lucid dreaming and peyote for inducing deep mystic states in his seminal 1970s books about shamanism.[9] All psychedelic drugs are known to induce states of lucid dreaming, and while psychologists are still arguing about whether regular marijuana use boosts or inhibits dreaming, I find general agreement among people using cannabis that it does increase their natural ability to experience lucid dream states. In his book *Dreaming Wide Awake: Lucid Dreaming, Shamanic Healing, and*

Psychedelics, David Jay Brown states that "being high on cannabis is actually dreamlike in some ways, and as such may serve a similar psychological function."[10]

For our focus on couples using cannabis together, I want to point out that in the last stage of a shared cannabis high, along with meditation, you can also indulge in focusing on whatever dream flows come to you. As you close your eyes and watch the show that so often comes effortlessly to the fore at this phase of the cannabis high, you don't need to do anything at all – except instead of falling asleep, choose to remain aware that you're dreaming while you dream.

You might also value a short guided introduction to this lucid dreaming experience. One of my early teachers in this regard, Rebecca Oriard, was the first to guide me through this process, so I'll give her credit and pass on her technique to you. The aim is to get you "aloft" and weightlessly sailing over a beautiful landscape (similar to the ancient Tibetan Buddhist preparation) . . . and then let you spontaneously land on your feet if and when you want to, anywhere that you might spontaneously choose, and set you free to lucidly dream whatever experience or adventure might come to you.

You are free to surrender to whatever your deeper realms of consciousness might bring to you, or you can also actively guide your own dream wherever you want. This is a learned ability, so experiment often and develop your own personal approach; you can also search online for a technique that suits you.[11]

You and your partner might choose to take turns guiding each other with this process. Remember that a dream is just a dream; you won't get hurt no matter what you dream is happening, and you can wake up and end the lucid dream anytime you want. Afterward, you'll perhaps want to take time to reflect on your experience and see whether any lucid realizations pop to the fore – this is an insight trip! And of course, share your experience with your partner.

Here's a basic guide into a high lucid dream state:

When you're ready, get comfortable in a recliner chair, bed, sofa, or whatever . . . and tune in to your breathing as usual . . . expand your awareness to include your head . . . your torso . . . your legs . . . your feet . . . and the earth under you.

Now begin to feel your body becoming lighter and lighter . . . and feel yourself becoming weightless . . . and you are beginning to float off the ground . . . and you are conscious that you are dreaming. . . .

Now imagine that you're outside on a warm springtime afternoon . . . floating . . . and as you feel the desire to rise up, let yourself actually feel your body like a great bird flapping its wings, taking you up high over the trees . . . and now you are soaring high on gentle breezes. . . .

Down below you are green trees and grassland . . . you see a stream running with clear, cool water down a valley, and you follow the stream from high above . . . you are free and happy . . . nowhere to go, nothing to do . . . and if you want to, you can begin looking for somewhere below that you'd really like to explore . . . and without any effort or forethought, if you want to, you can land on your own feet in that spot . . . and continue with your experience . . . staying aware that you're dreaming, even as your dream now unfolds as it wants to . . . you're in charge . . . see what comes to you now. . . .

Keeping the Adventure Alive

Here we sit,
high together,
straddling our celestial ball,
hurtling through infinity,
flying dauntlessly away from nothing,
through nothing, and
into nothing,
and yet here we sit,
taking it all so very seriously.
We speak of ourselves as a galaxy,
insignificant and very slight,
two random electrons
with perfect trajectory,
floating blissfully,
weightless,
through the vacuum
of our minds,
sharing love together,
eternally . . .

Getting high together is a great escape into mutual fun zones, and at the same time a long-term path into the infinite depths and heights of human love. One of the wonders of cannabis is that when it is approached properly, the experience never gets old – we can light up regularly with our beloved for a whole lifetime, and each time we will flow into a unique experience together. It's all about nurturing present-moment awareness and discovering new expressions of passion, fun, insight, and bonding.

I'd like to end this book with an exploration that I first thought I'd put in the beginning – a discussion of specific mind-set choices and themes that help couples keep newness alive. We've seen that focus is everything; where you aim your mind's attention each moment determines what happens. And when you both focus in the same direction, sharing naturally occurs.

Human cultures throughout history have agreed that there are core human values, principles, and virtues that express our best potential – and all we need to do in order to sustain a healthy evolving society is to focus our attention regularly toward these vital human virtues. This very act of holding our shared values and intentions in our minds will then naturally guide our lives and relationships in uplifting and sustainable directions.

From my studies in anthropology and history and my own meditations and explorations, I've found that there are about a dozen universal virtues and intentions that all humans seem to be born with. Perhaps they are encoded in our very genes; they certainly play a large role in our cultural heritage.

Given half a chance, these positive human qualities
sustain families, communities, nations, and cultures,
and they are always alive and available in
our hearts, minds, and souls.

Research has shown that the muse of marijuana actively helps to elicit these virtues each time we light up together: "Using brain imaging technology (fMRI), researchers were able to watch the effects of THC on the parts of the participants' brains that process emotion – identifying a network-wide shift from a bias for negative emotional content towards a bias for positive emotional content."[1]

"Positive emotional content" is a catchall psychological term referring to universal human feelings such as joy, hope, trust, compassion, cooperation, gentleness, patience, enthusiasm, confidence, humor, faith, thankfulness, courage, and love. Traditionally these are referred to as the human virtues. Each unique loving couple in the human race represents a primal dyad relationship that's founded, nurtured, and empowered by these core human virtues. They're what hold us together in community – and at least from my understanding, the more we hold them in mind when we are high together, the more we will expand their positive power in our lives.

The human virtues represent our core human goodness. Nothing in this book would make sense if we removed the basic assumption that goodness is the primary human virtue. What is love, after all, but the goodness of the human heart? Whether you're listening to Jesus or the Beatles, "Love is all you need."

Love is the earthly foundation of the creative harmony of
the universe. When love prevails, there's an uplift
in spirit; there's harmony rather than discord;
there's hope rather than despair.

All of the world's religions are founded on the premise that love is all there is.[2] Confucius and Krishna, Buddha and Jesus, Muhammad and Shankara, Aristotle and Plato, Saint Augustine and Thomas Aquinas, Baruch Spinoza and Carl Jung, Eric Fromm and, well, the Beatles . . . all put human love atop the highest pinnacle of what's most important in life. And if using marijuana aims us in loving directions, more power to it!

When interviewed, John Lennon put it this way: "Marijuana was the main thing that promoted non-violence amongst the youth. It's a community thing, and nothing on earth is going to stop it. The only thing to do is to find out how to use it for good."

When I was a kid, one particular quote about the priority of goodness and love from the Bible struck me to the quick, and even though I now consider myself a post-Christian (see my book *Jesus for the Rest of Us*), I still find this quote powerful:

Though I speak with the tongues of men and of angels, but have not love, I have become sounding brass or a clanging cymbal. And though I have the gift of prophecy, and understand all mysteries and all knowledge, but have not love, I am nothing. And though I bestow all my goods to feed the poor but have not love, it profits me nothing.

Love suffers long and is kind; love does not envy; love does not parade itself, it is not puffed up; it does not behave rudely, does not seek its own, is not provoked, it thinks no evil; does not rejoice in iniquity, but rejoices in the truth. Love bears all things, believes all things, hopes all things, endures all things.

Love never fails. . . . And now abide faith, hope, love, these three; but the greatest of these is love. (1 Corinthians 13:1)

TRUE LOVE AND HIGH VIRTUES

As I see it, when you get high with a lover or friend, be it platonic love or wild eros, you're both opening your heart to let love flow in. That's the great opportunity, the great choice, the great leap into something that transcends your ego and expands your experience of what life is all about. This whole book has been based on this same faith: that the muse of marijuana is grounded in love.

In his book *The Perennial Philosophy*, Aldous Huxley showed that human beings everywhere have expressed the same core virtues, all of them based on love and its various aspects and dimensions. In similar spirit, I'd like to share with you the fourteen primary virtues that seem to permeate our human striving toward goodness and love in the world. There are other lists, of course, and many variations on the virtue theme; this is simply my understanding and my list, and you should feel free to amend it as you wish.

On the High Together app (which you can find on the Mindfully High website), you'll find various methods that allow you to quickly tune in to one or more of these virtues so that you can effortlessly hold them in mind as you get high. If you're not sure where to start, on the app you can spin the Virtue Roulette Wheel and let the power of synchronicity deliver your "virtue of the day."

> In contrast to values and principles, virtues aren't just intellectual ideas or concepts for you to examine in your mind; they're actual energetically charged feelings that you experience as whole-body happenings.

As a prime example, you *feel* love. Love isn't a thing but an interior phenomenon felt in your heart and throughout your body. In fact, I would venture to say that it's through your interior sixth sense (the feeling of your own bodily presence, position, movement, pleasure, and emotion) that you experience all the primary virtues.

The name of each virtue (I'll offer two options for each one) will serve as an elicitor that aim your attention instantly inward to make contact with this particular good feeling in your body. In the overview of the fourteen virtues below, the description of each one concludes with a focus phrase that you can use to aim your mind's attention. Whenever you want to strengthen a virtue's presence within you, just hold this focus phrase in your mind as you go about your day or perhaps during a high session with your partner. Virtues naturally expand and gain prominence in your life when you you focus your attention in their direction – that's the key!

You might want to read through the list of virtues with your partner and share how you think and feel about each one, and how it impacts your relationship. Be sure to give the Virtue Roulette Wheel on the app a try when you are high. Many people feel that being high increases your sense of meaningful coincidence, so you can spin the wheel and allow the wisdom of synchronicity to guide you to your virtue for the day.[3]

On the following pages are the key "high virtues" that are also offered as audio on the High Together app.

The Fourteen Mindfully High Virtues

"I feel compassion in my heart. . . ."

◄o►

"I feel trustworthy. . . ."

◄o►

"I feel inclusive and cooperative. . . ."

◄o►

"I forgive myself and all others. . . ."

◄o►

"I live modestly in simplicity. . . ."

◄o►

"I feel patient and flexible. . . ."

◄o►

"I feel responsible for all my actions. . . ."

◄o►

"I feel sincere in my heart. . . ."

◄o►

"I feel tolerant and accepting. . . ."

◄o►

"I am faithful and humble. . . ."

◄o►

"I feel courageous and enthusiastic. . . ."

◄o►

"I feel thankful in my heart. . . ."

◄o►

"I strive to live every moment with integrity. . . ."

◄o►

"I feel balanced and fulfilled. . . ."

Expressing Compassion
. . . Connecting

Love is a whole-body feeling, and it's a two-step dance. With the first step, you choose to simply open your heart and let love flow in as you feel compassion for your own self. Then you let this infinite loving energy radiate outward to connect with all others. When you are high, you can direct your full attention first to your breathing and your heart as you connect more and more deeply with the infinite power and presence of love; then you can share this feeling by connecting heart-to-heart with your partner. You can't store compassion; it's energetic and can't be contained. You simply keep your heart open to receive compassion and then let it flow equally outward from your heart to connect energetically with the hearts of those around you.

Pause . . . close your eyes and tune in to your breaths coming and going . . . and then simply say the focus phrase below as a statement of inner intent . . . and let the elicitor words guide your attention directly toward actually experiencing the presence of the virtue alive within you, always awaiting your call.

"I feel compassion in my heart. . . ."

Feeling Trustworthy
...Honest

Akin to love, trust and honesty begin as feelings that you nurture in your own heart and mind, and then you allow these feelings to radiate outward. Most of us aren't completely trustworthy or honest all the time, but we certainly can aspire in that ultimate direction. As kids, we often had to choose between lying or punishment. As adults, we can realize that being dishonest is a terrible and disempowering feeling, whereas being honest and trusted is a wonderful and empowering stance. It's a great liberation to choose to be trustworthy – and the more you focus on that intent, the more trustworthy you become, enjoying a deep sense of wholeness and goodness. Focusing on the feeling of mutual trust when we are high with a partner generates an almost tangible bond that, in turn, leads to feelings of security and well-being.

Pause for a moment now . . . breathe into the feelings in your heart . . . and reflect a bit on how it feels to be trustworthy with those around you, to speak truth from the heart . . . tune in to the ease with which you can live when you make honesty a primary virtue . . . and now look at this focus phrase, read the words as an idea, and say the words from your heart:

"I feel trustworthy. . . ."

Being Cooperative
. . . Inclusive

Being exclusive and uncooperative – these are qualities and choices that don't feel good. They remind us of people who have a closed heart, who are disharmonious in their relationships, who express the habitual intent to shut others out. Being exclusive means being powered by fear, not love. In stark contrast, the virtue of cooperation represents the choice to open your heart, to create plenty of loving room for all feelings and all people. Just choosing to get along, to participate in rather than manipulate your relationship, is a major virtuous act. And when you feel inclusive, you discover that you have plenty of loving space to welcome others into your heart.

~~~

Reflect on the idea that it is always, with each new moment, your choice to open your heart to receive and give love and cooperation. A closed heart can hold no love, but an open heart can be filled instantly with infinite love. Press your palms together in front of you . . . and now open them, turn your palms upward, and move them outward to each side in a receiving gesture . . . and let the good feeling of including others in your heart flow in . . . and express that intent with these words:

~~~

"I feel inclusive and cooperative. . . ."

Relating Gently
... Forgiving

As with all the virtues, first you must relate gently with your own self. Forgive yourself for all the negative things you judge yourself for having done. Deciding to be kind and gentle rather than hard and blaming is a clear choice that you can make in each moment of your life, toward both yourself and your partner. When you become conscious of openly welcoming and activating this virtue, and at the same time you stay tuned in to your breathing and your heart's feelings, you will actively build this virtue as a core quality of who you are.

Blame as opposed to forgiveness is always a defensive posture. It benefits no one and damages intimacy. You'll find that when you're high with your partner, it's relatively easy to forgive and let go of relationship tensions and chronic blame of each other for past transgressions. And after a high session, you might want to continue exploring your blame reflex so that you can truly let it go and come to rest in the gentle open arms of forgiveness. . . .

"I forgive myself and all others. . . ."

Living Modestly
... Simplicity

This virtue seems to have been mostly lost in America; we are programmed to be flashy and to stuff our lives with as much wealth and complexity as we can. However, our recent cultural focus on being more mindful expresses the inherent wisdom that the virtue of modesty and simplicity is important, and it's a clear path to a more satisfying life. When we stop trying to impress the world with how great we are and choose to relax and enjoy a more modest and simple flow of daily life, we discover a primary key to fulfillment. When we are high together, we express this virtue in choosing to just simply "be" together, rather than constantly pushing to "do" something in search of satisfaction. Doing anything at all generates complexity and striving. Just simply being together, without having to do anything at all in order to feel content – this is the magic and essence of simplicity!

Imagine for a few moments that you actually feel good and complete and satisfied right now inside your own skin, without needing to do or have anything at all ... breathe into this feeling of simplicity and contentment ... and now say the following words several times to yourself, and feel how the words resonate within you:

"I live modestly in simplicity. . . ."

Being Adaptable
. . . Patient

In our thoughts as well as our actions, we can all too easily become rigid and unbending, impatient and refusing to give way or to change. But fighting against change, or being impatient when things don't go your way, is a sure formula for dissatisfaction and failure. You'll find that when you get high with your partner, you'll have the opportunity to stop resisting and insisting on your own way when you have disagreement. Instead, you always have the freedom to peacefully give ground and seek to find win-win compromise. This in turn leads to harmony between you and peace in your heart.

Whenever you can, patiently observe your impatience when it rises up inside you . . . and purposefully act to put the impatience aside. Breathe into letting this present moment unfold gracefully on its own rather than trying to hurry things up. Be willing to do something new and different rather than insisting on having everything your own way. Being adaptable is surely a virtue, and patience, as they say, is golden!

"I feel patient and flexible. . . ."

Acting Responsibly
. . . Diligence

Being responsible is often left off the list of human virtues, but it's vital for nurturing the full sense of living a good life. Maintaining due diligence means actively caring for the unfolding of each new moment. It implies staying aware and alert to what's happening and responding in ways that augment rather than disturb the situation. Diligence is similar to being honest and trustworthy; it means that you feel an inherent responsibility to oversee a situation and to act in ways that nurture harmony, well-being, and success for everyone involved. Certainly staying fully responsible is a key virtue when you get high; you may be unexpectedly called on to exert extra diligence as you merge being high with being responsible at the same time.

〜〜〜

When you pay close attention to what's happening around and within you, without judging or manipulating, you spontaneously know in your heart when and how to act responsibly. Rather than doing what you think you should or want to, always strive to do what you feel is right and correct.

〜〜〜

"I feel responsible for all my actions. . . ."

Remaining Innocent
. . . Sincere

Feeling innocent implies that you are not secretly plotting to manipulate a situation to your own advantage. When you're feeling sincere, you're expressing a clarity of intention and an openness to engage in fair interaction. You're not "up to something" – instead, you're surrendering sincerely to the needs of the moment. Cannabis often reinforces this virtue of innocence and sincerity, allowing you to let go of being devious and instead act directly from the goodness of your heart. Then your partner can respond to your sincerity with the same spontaneous spirit of trust and shared engagement. Remember the feeling you had as a child, when you woke up in the morning and smiled? It's time to feel like that again!

Children can be innocent and sincere because they haven't learned how to be devious and manipulative. You do still have that innocent reflex inside you, and you can tap into it – especially when you are high. Just use the following focus phrase to best advantage. Say it often, hold it in your mind and heart, and express it as a core feeling toward your loved one.

"I feel sincere in my heart. . . ."

Spreading Tolerance
... Accepting

The thinking mind is great at judging and rejecting; this is the ego's main fear-based protective pattern for moving you through life. But when there's anxiety and critique in the mind, there can be no love in the heart. One of the blessings of the marijuana muse is that when you get high, you'll probably find that your mind tends to ease up and be more accepting. Research has clarified that cannabis does make most people feel temporarily more accepting and tolerant. And true spiritual leaders have always encouraged us to "judge not" and to "love one another." The trick is to stop being afraid and threatened by others, and instead to hold the feeling of tolerance in your heart.

~~~

When you are high with your partner, you'll find that it's actually much easier to let go of any need to judge their actions or intentions. The same is true when it comes to judging yourself. Let it all go. Choose to embody the virtue of tolerance for yourself and your partner, and you will expand into a feeling of everything being perfectly okay in your life. Acceptance leads to relief!

~~~

"I feel tolerant and accepting. . . ."

Staying Faithful
. . . Humble

As you can see, most virtues deal with relationships – your relationship with your own self and with others. Virtues are intended to maximize personal, family, and community harmony and sustainability. In this spirit, being faithful isn't based on vows and obligations, it's evoked by honoring and cherishing the relationships you've chosen to engage in. And being humble means being satisfied with who you naturally are and what has come to you, rather than chasing off after more lofty things and relationships. If you are faithful to your own self and stay immersed in the power and spirit of love rather than insecure ego needs and distractions, living within the virtue of faithfulness is as natural as love itself.

~~~

When you're high, you can consciously choose to expand this feeling of "being humbly present" for your partner. This generates a wonderful sense of peace, security, and caring. Both faithfulness and humility begin in your own heart and your devotion to your own ongoing spiritual evolution. When you focus your attention on these qualities in yourself, you can watch how your inner sense of devotion naturally radiates outward to embrace your partner.

~~~

"I am faithful and humble. . . ."

Becoming Courageous
. . . Enthusiastic

The twin qualities of courage and enthusiasm are often left off the virtues list, but I consider them to be core positive feelings that help sustain all of us and our world community. You can notice that when you're not feeling enthusiastic about your relationship, for instance, there is a negative energetic drag on that relationship. And if you don't feel courageous in relating, your relationship can die for lack of exploration, risk, and adventure. Nurturing this inner sense of exploration, fearlessness, and enthusiasm is a choice that you're making all the time – but only if you remember to do it! So in the face of worry and uncertainty and doubt, shift your focus to feeling pure courage and enthusiasm, and take that essential leap into the new!

〜〜

I encourage you to regularly call anxiety's bluff by courageously saying the word enthusiasm *to yourself, especially when you are high with your partner, so that you direct your power of attention toward expanding the root human challenge of moving through life with courage in your heart.*

〜〜

"I feel courageous and enthusiastic. . . ."

Expressing Gratitude
... Thankful

A lot of us got turned off to the word *gratitude* because we were told as children that we had to be grateful for what we had or else we were bad. But gratitude is a feeling that can't be forced, no more than any other virtue can be forced into being. Gratitude is a response of the heart spontaneously opening. When we observe that someone has done something kind and generous toward us, or that the world in general has smiled on us, we feel a natural response in our heart that expresses the deep good feeling of thankfulness.

⌇

Especially when you are high, you can pause often and reflect on your present-moment situation – you're alive on an amazing planet, you have a partner to share your life with, you're living in a free country where you can pursue your heart's delight. There's loads to feel spontaneously thankful for if you pause and take notice of all your blessings. When you're high with your partner, you'll find that if you bring this gratitude virtue to mind, you'll open a bright feeling in your heart that will then flow outward. By saying to your partner something like, "I feel lucky just being with you like this," you awaken the feeling and share it – and it feels good!

⌇

"I feel thankful in my heart. . . ."

Remaining Transparent
... Integrity

In childhood you probably had to hide a lot of your spontaneous feelings and impulses; you had to put on a mask and
pretend to have feelings that weren't genuine. You became inau-
thentic, like all of us did, which is an unavoidable part of the
human socialization process. However, you also have the choice
as an adult to decide to stop being phony and instead to feel
and act with integrity in all that you do. This is so important
in a relationship, and especially when you are high with your
partner. If you're authentic, everything seems to flow easily in
a relationship because you're not trying to hide any part of you.

*Rather than concealing and hiding how you really feel
about something, you can choose to risk being seen and
dare to be transparent. Especially when you are high
with your partner, activating this virtue of integrity and
authenticity will generate a remarkable deepening, soft-
ening, and sharing quality between the two of you. And
all you need to do to be authentic is to regularly tune in
to your breathing, admit to all your feelings, and live
from your vulnerable heart, not your ego identity.*

"I strive to live every moment with integrity. . . ."

Staying Balanced
... Fulfilled

We live in a binary universe of dark and light, high and low, in and out, off and on, hot and cold, and so on. When we get out of balance in any dimension, things tend to misfire. When we swing to one extreme, often we must swing to the other extreme to find balance. Our bodies know how to stay in balance with our blood pressure, saline content, biochemical ratios, oxygen–carbon dioxide balance, and so forth. We also have our physical sense of balance (the sixth sense). And as we've seen, when we are high, finding a happy balance between talking and listening, thinking and being quiet, moving and being still is important. When you're high, there's a tendency to indulge and overdo things, but it's vital to return regularly to a sense of inner balance. When you're feeling in balance at all levels, you can relax and feel a deep sense of calm fulfillment.

~~~

It's a blessing to those around you when you choose to stay aware of your own inner balance and gently return to a state of equilibrium, equanimity, and homeostasis. Balancing spontaneity and moderation empowers a relationship to grow and explore while also staying calm and centered. Mutual fulfillment emerges step-by-step by nurturing this shared virtue of balance, equanimity, and well-being.

~~~

"I feel balanced and fulfilled. . . ."

Similar to the de-beliefing process we discussed in chapter 9, these Mindfully High virtues help reprogram your subconscious mind with the positive themes and intentions that you hold to be most important to your life. The more you make the effort to return to this list and to hold one or more of these virtues in your mind all through a day, the deeper this transformative process will become.

As you go about your daily routines, you'll find that a negative one-liner will suddenly be present in your conscious mind, seeping up through a crack between your conscious and subconscious realms of awareness. Every time a negative one-liner pops up, try to write it down. Then come up with its exact opposite, and write that down. Take this pair of opposite one-liners with you into your next shared high experience, and go through the de-beliefing process openly with your partner.

You can, of course, come up with additional things to do during any stage of a new shared-high experience. Feel free to visit the Mindfully High website in order to use the High Together app, where we'll be regularly posting new suggestions and guided programs, and to tap into our Cannabis for Couples community to share your experiences and insights. It's been my pleasure sharing the programs in this book with you!

The Free High Together App

As mentioned throughout this book, the author and his Mindfully High organization has produced a free High Together app that you can install and integrate into your Cannabis for Couples experiences, on either Apple or Android mobile devices. Most of the guided sessions offered in this book are available in extended audio formats on the app.

You'll also find many other features and experiences to enhance your high experience, whether on your own or with your partner: Surprise Spin, Audio Guidance, Primal Journeys, Video Uplifts, Mind Games, Insight Photos, High Together Journal and Favorites – and much more.

To install the free High Together app, and for more information about couples using cannabis together, please visit us at the Mindfully High website: www.mindfullyhigh.com/app.

Online Guidance & Community

Please feel free to join us often at our Cannabis for Couples and Mindfully High website for audio and video guidance, inspirational suggestions and insights, book and media reviews, community chats, and much more. We welcome your ideas and stories and look forward to seeing you in our various online circles at www.mindfullyhigh.com.

Notes

Note to readers: Because hyperlinks do not always remain viable, please be aware that some of the references listed below may no longer be available to view.

INTRODUCTION.
HOW CANNABIS ENHANCES INTIMACY

1. https://home.liebertpub.com/publications/cannabis-and-cannabinoid -research/633/overview.
2. https://www.huffpost.com/entry/molson-coors-marijuana-beer_n _5b3145e8e4b0b745f176fab1.
3. https://www.med.stanford.edu/news/all-news/2017/10/regular-marijuana -use-linked-to-more-sex.html.
4. https://www.civilized.life/articles/couples-who-smoke-together-stay -together-according-to-cannabis-study.
5. http://druglibrary.org/schaffer/hemp/general/mjeff1.htm.
6. https://psychedelictimes.com/giving-psychedelic-meaning-5-fascinating -things-about-humphry-osmond-the-man-who-invented-the-word -psychedelic.
7. https://en.wikipedia.org/wiki/Cannabis_use_disorder.

CHAPTER ONE.
MEET THE MARIJUANA MUSE

1. https://en.wikipedia.org/wiki/Humphry_Osmond.
2. https://en.wikipedia.org/wiki/Indian_Hemp_Drugs_Commission.

3. https://www.thegospelcoalition.org/article/is-recreational-marijuana
-use-a-sin.

CHAPTER TWO.
CLUES FROM THE RESEARCH TRAIL

1. https://www.civilized.life/articles/scientists-say-marijuana-research-has-an
-anti-cannabis-bias.
2. https://sencanada.ca/content/sen/committee/371/ille/rep/summary
-e.pdf.
3. https://en.wikipedia.org/wiki/Cannabis.
4. https://www.tokeofthetown.com/wp-content/uploads/2011/08/photo
-5.jpeg.
5. http://www.madehow.com/Volume-6/Industrial-Hemp.html.
6. https://www.theatlantic.com/health/archive/2013/12/religion-as-a
-product-of-psychotropic-drug-use/282484.
7. https://www.ncbi.nlm.nih.gov/pmc/articles/PMC3736954.
8. https://www.britannica.com/science/tetrahydrocannabinol;
https://en.wikipedia.org/wiki/Cannabidiol.
9. https://www.vox.com/2014/9/25/6842187/drug-schedule-list
-marijuana.
10. https://www.cannabisculture.com/content/2006/04/13/4721.
11. https://en.wikipedia.org/wiki/Cannabis_dispensaries_in_the_United
_States; https://en.wikipedia.org/wiki/Black_market.
12. https://en.wikipedia.org/wiki/Hashish.
13. https://en.wikipedia.org/wiki/Tincture_of_cannabis.
14. https://en.wikipedia.org/wiki/Effects_of_cannabis.
15. https://www.businessinsider.com/cannabis-marijuana-psychedelic-drug
-why-2017-7.
16. https://www.hellomd.com/health-wellness/58ac759d05b7950007646b95
/how-to-stop-a-marijuana-induced-anxiety-attack.
17. https://herb.co/learn/happens-liver-eat-edibles.
18. https://hightimes.com/culture/people/the-man-who-discovered-thc.
19. http://cannabis.uci.edu/bio/allyn-howlett.
20. http://www.marijuanatimes.org/the-endocannabinoid-system-a-history
-of-endocannabinoids-and-cannabis.

21. https://www.allbud.com/learn/story/how-effects-eating-cannabis-differ
-smoking-it.
22. https://www.leafly.com/news/cannabis-101/differences-between-marijuana
-edibles-and-flower.
23. https://www.bustle.com/articles/115782-8-side-effects-of-getting-high
-explained.
24. https://potent.media/how-weed-affects-your-5-senses.
25. https://www.wikileaf.com/thestash/thc-cause-hallucinations.
26. https://www.vice.com/en_us/article/aey385/what-mixing-weed-and
-alcohol-does-to-your-mind.
27. https://www.cnn.com/2013/08/08/health/gupta-changed-mind
-marijuana/index.html.
28. https://www.allbud.com/learn/story/cannabis-and-our-cognitive-abilities
-do-people-pre.
29. https://www.marijuanamoment.net/smoking-marijuana-actually
-improves-working-memory-study-indicates.
30. https://www.mic.com/articles/166394/marijuana-anxiety-heres-what
-to-do-if-you-have-a-panic-attack-while-high#.GpuyuiGMY.
31. https://en.wikipedia.org/wiki/Reefer_Madness.
32. https://www.leafly.com/news/health/cannabis-induced-psychosis-real
-or-reefer-madness.
33. http://healthland.time.com/2012/01/10/study-smoking-marijuana-not
-linked-with-lung-damage.
34. https://www.ukcia.org/research/PhysioPsychoEffects.pdf.
35. https://norml.org/pdf_files/testimony/NORML_WA_Driving
_Presentation.pdf.
36. https://norml.org/library/item/marijuana-and-driving-a-review-of-the
-scientific-evidence.
37. https://www.sciencedaily.com/releases/2013/05/130530132531
.htm.
38. https://www.verywellmind.com/is-marijuana-addictive-67792.
39. https://www.medicalnewstoday.com/articles/324301.php.
40. https://www.drugabuse.gov/publications/drugfacts/understanding-drug
-use-addiction.

CHAPTER THREE.
COUPLES CHOOSING CANNABIS

1. https://en.wikipedia.org/wiki/LGBT_demographics_of_the_United _States.
2. https://www.leafly.com/news/health/cannabis-and-pregnancy-what-does -the-science-say.

CHAPTER FOUR.
PREPARING TO TAKE OFF TOGETHER

1. https://www.summitdaily.com/news/marijuana-vessels-joints-pipes-bongs -bats-and-other-ways-to-smoke.
2. https://www.leafly.com/news/science-tech/cannabis-science-101-the -complex-chemistry-of-the-bong-b2ce.
3. https://www.summitdaily.com/news/marijuana-vessels-joints-pipes-bongs -bats-and-other-ways-to-smoke.
4. https://www.leafly.com/news/strains-products/the-best-dab-rig-for-any -situation.
5. http://www.leafly.com/news/cannabis101/the-complete-list-of -cannabis-delivery-methods; http://www.leafly.com/news/cannabis101 /the-great-wide-world-of-cannabis-concentrates.
6. http://www.leafly.com/news/cannabis101/what-are-cannabis-dabs-and -benefits.
7. http://www.maximumyield.com/definition/4776/dry-herb-vaporizer.
8. https://www.leafly.com/news/strains-products/what-are-pre-filled-cannabis -oil-vape-cartridges.
9. https://coloradocannabistours.com/guides/concentrates-oil-wax-dabs.
10. http://www.inverse.com/article/58581-dank-vapes.
11. https://honestmarijuana.com/marijuana-tinctures.
12. http://en.wikipedia.org./wiki/history-of-medical-cannabis#modern -history.
13. https://www.ncbi.nlm.nih.gov/pmc/articles/PMC5260817.
14. https://dailyburn.com/life/lifestyle/cannabis-edibles-health-effects -420.

15. https://www.royalqueenseeds.com/blog-can-you-ever-mix-alcohol-with
    -cannabis-n640.
16. https://www.vice.com/en_us/article/aey385/what-mixing-weed-and
    -alcohol-does-to-your-mind; https://www.occnewspaper.com
    /alcohol-and-cannabis-the-science-behind-how-they-interact.
17. http://www.yogajournal.com/practice/reclining-bound-angle-pose.
18. https://sebastianmarincolo.wordpress.com/2012/02/15/marijuana-insights
    -myth-or-reality.

CHAPTER FIVE.
TAPPING INTO THE MAGIC

1. https://www.the-scientist.com/features/your-body-is-teeming-with
   -weed-receptors-31233.
2. https://www.sciencealert.com/the-way-you-breath-could-change-your
   -emotions.
3. https://www.ncbi.nlm.nih.gov/pmc/articles/PMC5877694.
4. https://networkmagazine.ie/articles/breath-life-link-between-breathing
   -and-emotions.

CHAPTER SIX.
FINESSING THE CHATTERBOX PHASE

1. http://www.johnselby.com/quiet-mind.
2. https://greencamp.com/why-does-weed-make-you-laugh.
3. https://www.gaiam.com/blogs/discover/7-health-benefits-of-laughter.
4. http://radix.org/; http://www.londonradix.com/reich-and-kelley.

CHAPTER SEVEN.
COMING FULLY TO YOUR SENSES

1. https://420intel.com/articles/2018/10/02/how-cannabis-affects-five-senses.
2. www.yourhormones.info/hormones/ghrelin.
3. https://www.vox.com/2015/1/28/7925737/touch-facts.
4. http://www.labroots.com/trending/cannabis-sciences/13150/meet
   -amandamine-bliss-molecule.

5. http://www.vice.com/en_us/article/3dea3k/420-music-weed-expert.

6. https://www.thegrowthop.com/cannabis-culture/music-your-brain-and
-cannabis-not-what-you-think.

7. https://www.livescience.com/57148-does-marijuana-use-affect-retinal
-cells.html.

8. http://www.fifthsense.org.uk/psychology-and-smell/; https://www.ncbi
.nlm.nih.gov/pubmed/19134495.

9. http://en.wikipedia.org/wiki/anosmia.

10. http://www.fifthsense.org.uk/psychology-and-smell.

11. http://www.7senses.org.au/what-are-the-7-senses.

CHAPTER EIGHT.
TAPPING EROS TRANSFORMATION

1. https://medicalxpress.com/news/2018-10-pot-sexual-desire-science
.html.

2. https://med.stanford.edu/news/all-news/2017/10/regular-marijuana
-use-linked-to-more-sex.html.

3. https://www.psychologytoday.com/us/blog/all-about-sex/201808/the
-largest-best-studies-yet-sex-and-marijuana.

4. https://www.bbc.com/news/newsbeat-47787138.

5. https://www.yogiapproved.com/yoga/cannabis-yoga.

6. http://www.ganjayoga.com.

7. https://www.leafly.com/news/health/sexy-flex-tantra-yoga-plus-cannabis
-of-course.

8. http://www.embodiment.net.

9. https://en.wikipedia.org/wiki/Reefer_Madness.

10. https://www.sciencedirect.com/science/article/pii/037687169190068A.

11. https://www.psychologytoday.com/us/blog/all-about-sex/201003/how
-does-marijuana-affect-your-sex-life.

12. https://www.self.com/gallery/how-cannabis-affects-sex.

13. https://www.vice.com/en_us/article/8xmqmk/this-edible-wants-to
-improve-your-sex-life.

14. https://en.wikipedia.org/wiki/Wilhelm_Reich.

15. https://www.verywellhealth.com/what-is-outercourse-3132810.

16. https://en.wikipedia.org/wiki/Masturbation.

17. http://www.naturalwellness.com/nwupdate/solo-love-has-heart -benefits.

18. https://www.leafly.com/news/health/how-opioids-marijuana-work -together-for-pain-relief.

19. https://en.wikipedia.org/wiki/Alan_Watts.

20. https://jkrishnamurti.org.

CHAPTER NINE.
SHARING NEW CREATIVE INSIGHTS

1. https://www.planet13lasvegas.com/2018/10/13/high-end-imagination -cannabis-and-creativity.

2. https://patch.com/california/santacruz/does-cannabis-boost-creativity.

3. https://www.psychologytoday.com/us/blog/psychology-masala/201204 /cannabis-and-creativity.

4. http://www.green-flower.com/articles/577/cannabis-and-creativity.

5. https://www.leafly.com/news/science-tech/cannabis-and-creativity -science.

6. http://www.green-flower.com/articles/577/cannabis-and-creativity.

CHAPTER TEN.
MUTUAL AWAKENING

1. https://www.marijuanabreak.com/how-long-does-weed-stay-in-your-system -full-explanation.

2. https://www.quora.com/What-types-of-trips-are-most-common-on -weed.

3. https://anthrosource.onlinelibrary.wiley.com/doi/pdf/10.1525/ac.2006 .17.2.78.

4. https://moniquechapman.com/cannabis-and-spirituality.

5. https://www.sciencealert.com/why-some-people-get-skin-orgasms-chills -from-listening-to-music-science.

6. https://en.wikipedia.org/wiki/Lucid_dream.

7. https://en.wikipedia.org/wiki/Dream_yoga.

8. https://en.wikipedia.org/wiki/Lucid_dream#Ancient.

9. http://en.wikipedia.org/wiki/Carlos_Castaneda.

10. http://hightimes.com/culture/is-lucid-dreaming-the-ultimate-high.

11. http://blog.mindvalley.com/lucid-dreaming-resources.

FINAL WORDS.
KEEPING THE ADVENTURE ALIVE

1. http://www.reinventingorganizations.com.

2. https://integralchurch.wordpress.com/2012/07/10/15-great-principles -shared-by-all-religions.

3. https://www.psychologytoday.com/us/blog/connecting-coincidence.

Index

About the Author

John Selby grew up on cattle ranches in Arizona and California. He graduated from Princeton University with a degree in psychology, received his doctorate degree from the Graduate Theological Union (at the University of California at Berkeley) and the San Francisco Theological Seminary, and completed his therapy training at the Radix Institute.

John conducted mind research for the National Institutes of Health with Humphry Osmond, MD, and studied traditional meditation techniques with Kriyananda, Alan Watts, Osho, and Krishnamurti. During a five-year stay in Europe, John directed experimental wellness programs with his European mentor, Manfred von Luhmann, MD. He also spent several years studying traditional mindfulness methods with native tribes in Mexico, South Africa, and Guatemala. Working as pastoral therapist for the San Rafael Presbyterian Church and then in private practice, John has helped clients integrate mindful marijuana use into their everyday lives.

John is the author of two dozen books on meditation and personal growth, plus a dozen novels and screenplays. Happily married with three sons, he lives in Santa Cruz. He recently worked with Plantronics and WizeWell to develop at-work mindfulness apps and programs. While still overseeing the Mindfully High program, John is currently completing a new novel and screenplay, while also mentoring new authors and doing cannabis phone-consulting and personal guidance sessions for readers of this book. For a personal phone conversation with John, please visit www.johnselby.com.

For more information about the author, please visit
www.johnselby.com and **www.mindfullyhigh.com.**

BOOKS OF RELATED INTEREST

Cannabis and Spirituality
An Explorer's Guide to an Ancient Plant Spirit Ally
Edited by Stephen Gray
Foreword by Julie Holland, M.D.

Cannabis in Spiritual Practice
The Ecstasy of Shiva, the Calm of Buddha
by Will Johnson

The Pot Book
A Complete Guide to Cannabis
by Julie Holland, M.D.

Marijuana Medicine
A World Tour of the Healing and Visionary Powers of Cannabis
by Christian Rätsch

Plants of the Gods
Their Sacred, Healing, and Hallucinogenic Powers
by Richard Evans Schultes, Albert Hofmann,
and Christian Rätsch

The Encyclopedia of Psychoactive Plants
Ethnopharmacology and Its Applications
by Christian Rätsch
Foreword by Albert Hofmann

The Psychedelic Explorer's Guide
Safe, Therapeutic, and Sacred Journeys
by James Fadiman, Ph.D.

Psychedelic Medicine
The Healing Powers of LSD, MDMA, Psilocybin, and Ayahuasca
by Dr. Richard Louis Miller

INNER TRADITIONS • BEAR & COMPANY
P.O. Box 388 • Rochester, VT 05767
1-800-246-8648 • www.InnerTraditions.com

Or contact your local bookseller